The History of the Laboratory Schools

THE
HISTORY
OF THE
LABORATORY
SCHOOLS

The University of Chicago
1896–1965

BY

Ida B. DePencier

Chicago | Quadrangle Books | 1967

Library of Congress Catalog Card Number: 67-12354

To Roy A. Larmee
*without whose interest, support,
and encouragement the research
for this book would not have
been undertaken*

I wish to acknowledge my indebtedness to friends and former colleagues who gave of their time for personal interviews, who provided information and archives material, and who read and made suggestions on parts of the manuscript.

To the parents whose interest in the Laboratory Schools led to the rewriting of this history, my thanks.

Contents

The History of the Laboratory Schools

One

The Beginnings

An event which was destined to have a profound effect on educational thinking and practice throughout America took place at the University of Chicago in January 1896. That event was the opening of the Dewey School, now known as the Laboratory Schools of the University of Chicago. Both names are appropriate. Conceived by the world-famous educator, John Dewey, the school was truly a laboratory from its inception—an experimental school where his theories of education could be put into practice, tested, and scientifically evaluated. Mr. Dewey had come to the University of Chicago in the summer of 1894, as head of the departments of Philosophy, Psychology, and Pedagogy. In the fall of 1895, the University appropriated a thousand dollars to establish the educational laboratory he so earnestly desired. Only a few months later the school began operation at 5714 Kimbark Avenue with about a dozen pupils, from six to nine years of age, two teachers, and an instructor who was listed as "in charge of manual training."

THE FERMENT

While John Dewey has been credited with bringing on a pedagogical revolution almost singlehanded, he himself had doubtless been influenced by the educational ferment which had started in Europe in the eighteenth century as a protest against prevailing educational methods.

One of the educational pioneers in the movement was Johann Heinrich Pestalozzi. In 1774, on a farm in Switzerland, Pestalozzi established a school for needy boys and girls. Besides their regular lessons, the boys learned to farm and the girls to cook and sew. In addition, both boys and girls were taught to spin and weave and thus help support the school. Visitors were impressed by Pestalozzi's kindness to the children, by the big-family atmosphere that pervaded the school, and above all by the happiness of the children in learning by doing.

Pestalozzi's first school had to be given up because of lack of funds, but he began again and for twenty years maintained a second school. Again many visitors came, but his ideas spread slowly. However, as time went on, Pestalozzi's influence increased, especially in England and the United States. There some educators, following his pioneering practices, began to break away from the formal, strongly verbal methods of the past, which emphasized quiet, passive absorption of book-imprisoned learning.

A German contemporary of Pestalozzi, Friedrich Froebel, was completely in sympathy with his revolutionary educational philosophy. Froebel, too, believed in learning through activity, but he went still further. He believed that play was an important factor in the child's education. He added to the ferment by organizing a *kindergarten,* or children's garden, where children learned through activity and play. His ideas were eagerly espoused in England, France, and especially in the United States, where many kindergartens were established.

Certain American educators during this same era focused their attention on children and how children learn. Horace Mann, who has been called the "father of American public education," without doubt was influenced by Froebel and Pestalozzi. One of his strong protests was against what he termed the "harsh pedagogy of the classroom." G. Stanley Hall, a contemporary and a one-time teacher of John Dewey, established the first institute of child psychology in the United States and one of the first psychological laboratories.

Chicago was not without men who contributed to the ferment. Chief among them was Colonel Francis Wayland Parker, a man of magnetic personality, forcefulness, and what one writer calls "a pathetic and intense sympathy for all children." He was born in New England and taught school there. When the War Between the States began, he enlisted in the Union Army, and before the war was over he was commissioned a colonel. He once told a friend that during his army service he used to spend his evenings thinking about teaching, wondering how school could be made a living, challenging experience for children instead of a dull, boring prison. After the war, he went to Germany for three years to study, and there came in contact with the teachings of Pestalozzi and Froebel.

On his return to the United States in 1875, Colonel Parker became superintendent of schools in Quincy, Massachusetts. What he did there was so new and exciting that teachers came from near and far to visit his schools—thirty thousand of them from 1875 to 1878. What was it that brought them in such numbers? An almost complete reversal of previous teaching methods.

The History of the Laboratory Schools

Colonel Parker was convinced that the strict formalism of the schools was not in keeping with children's needs. Self-development, he believed, was of primary importance, and a child should grow naturally and freely, learning by doing rather than being fettered by a desk and seat. He infected his teachers with his fervent interest in each child as a person, and their enthusiasm took the drudgery out of teaching the three R's. Pupils interspersed work with activity; learning came from the outdoors as well as from books. Geography, history, and nature study were the central unifying subjects, and other studies were correlated with these. Geography, for example, was no longer a dull memorizing of facts about places, but an effort to understand the whole physical world.

Colonel Parker seemed to know intuitively that children would learn happily and well about things they were interested in, things that came nearest to their own experiences. He based his methods on this principle, though it took high courage to break away from existing school practices. The success of his work at Quincy brought him national renown.

In 1883, he took the position of principal of the Cook County Normal School in Chicago. The training of teachers, he felt, was the best means of spreading the gospel of activity and freedom—freedom for both children and teachers. In his eighteen years as principal of the Normal School he built a faculty which was not afraid to experiment or to introduce innovations, and most of all a faculty greatly interested in childhood education.

Again his ideas reached a wide audience. At his "practice school," visiting teachers and even persons outside the teaching profession could see those ideas in operation. His published *Course of Study,* which included descriptions of materials, devices, and methods, had wide circulation and affected the classroom practices of hundreds of public school teachers.

Another Chicago man who added to the ferment was Henry Holmes Belfield. In 1883, the year Colonel Parker came to Chicago, Belfield opened a manual training school at Twelfth Street and Michigan Avenue. The school was established by the Commercial Club of Chicago, a group of influential businessmen dissatisfied with high school education in the city. Their chief objection was that high schools did not make sufficient use of students' touch, sight, and muscular sense, that classwork consisted largely of listening and memorizing—a process so dull that it often defeated learning. Belfield's school and other manual training schools covered the subjects in the high school curriculum but trained the hands as well as the head.

Thus in the latter part of the nineteenth century, education was in a state of ferment activated by enlightened, imaginative leaders who believed that children, in order to learn, needed freedom—freedom to move about, to investigate, to inquire, to experiment. This freedom was not wild and uncontrolled. On the contrary, it was freedom with discipline, discipline imposed by the child's interest, his bent, his self-direction. For the teachers who grasped the real meaning of this new freedom, there was joy in teaching—a deep satisfaction which matched the children's own happiness in school. And for the children they taught, school was no longer a repining misery.

To many adults, however, it was unthinkable that children should actually enjoy school. They misunderstood the real meaning of freedom to learn, and their misunderstanding later brought ill repute to the new teaching methods. Yet slowly, in small ways, these methods penetrated classrooms here and there, changing practices or philosophy. At the present time, most of what the pioneer proponents advocated has been incorporated into elementary school teaching, especially in the primary grades.

THE DEWEY SCHOOL

The Dewey School was wholly experimental, founded as a testing ground for John Dewey's educational theories. As Mr. Dewey himself put it in an address before the Pedagogical Club,

> The conception underlying the school is that of a laboratory. . . . It has two main purposes: (1) to exhibit, test, verify and criticize theoretical statements and principles, (2) to add to the sum of facts and principles in its special line. (*The University Record*, I, No. 32, 417.)

Mr. Dewey's school differed from Colonel Parker's, though both were experimental, because Colonel Parker was conducting a practice school where student teachers were trained. To be sure, his faculty members experimented with methods of teaching and certainly were innovators, but the two schools were fundamentally different. Colonel Parker knew *what* would help children learn; he did not know *why*. Mr. Dewey, with his keen philosophic insight, knew why. Colonel Parker once said that he and John Dewey shared the same ideas but that Mr. Dewey could express these ideas in philosophic terms. He also said that Mr. Dewey spoke for him better than he could speak for himself. Colonel

The Beginnings

Parker could not tell in any intellectually convincing way why he thought as he did; he knew intuitively what would work.

Each man added to the sum of knowledge about effective teaching. Colonel Parker made his contribution through his *Course of Study* and through the teachers whom he trained and inspired and who in turn taught and inspired other teachers. He was not a voluminous writer, and he spoke with difficulty, owing to a throat wound received in the battle at Petersburg. His success was due to his great human interest and sympathy, his magnetic personality, and his enthusiasm. Mr. Dewey was less magnetic but keenly analytical.

"It is sometimes thought," wrote John Dewey in 1899, "that the school started out with a number of ready made principles and ideas which were put into practice at once. . . . The teachers started out with question marks and if any answers have been reached, it is the teachers in the school who have supplied them." (*School and Society,* page 115.)

Perhaps the principles were not ready-made nor the ideas put into immediate practice, but principles and ideas there were, and they became evident in the practices of the school. Not all of them are indicated here, but some of them are as follows:

First, there was to be no break between the child's home activities and his first contact with the school. He was to be introduced to the school through activities connected with the home as a center of shelter, protection, comfort, and food supply—through handwork (manual training), cooking, and sewing—and from these he would gain social experience. Reading, writing, arithmetic, and spelling would come later, growing out of his need to get information and communicate with

19

others. He would begin by learning to prepare and cook his noonday lunch, to sew, and to construct needed materials by sawing, planing, and nailing. He would learn through experience—free to move about, communicate with others, and get help from the teacher and from his classmates. Mr. Dewey held that when a child was using a saw or plane it was not necessary to concoct artificial ways of holding his attention. His senses were already on the alert, since he must use them in order to do something. This was the psychological reason for starting the child's education with activities.

The home activities would form a basis for number work because measurement was constantly required in cooking, in carpentry, and in sewing. Thus arithmetic would be taught as a means through which some activity could be made more orderly and effective. Reading, writing, and spelling would be taught incidentally, as an outgrowth of the child's activities and his need to communicate.

Second, the child would learn to live in the present rather than preparing for adult life in the future. He would learn to be part of a group, taking his turn, helping his co-workers as well as getting help from them and from his teacher. The school would be a community in which the child had a responsible role, instead of just a place for learning lessons from a book. His feelings of success came from being a part of a cooperative enterprise instead of being the winner in a competitive field. One of the weaknesses of the schools of that time, John Dewey believed, was that they tried to prepare pupils for social living in a situation where, he stated in *School and Society,* "the conditions of social spirit are eminently wanting."

Third, the school was to be a place where the child's

curiosity would be aroused by problems, where he would be challenged to find solutions by his own methods as far as possible, using his own inventiveness and creativity. There was to be no rote learning, no answers to be committed to memory. Quite possibly the child would use considerable time in trial and error before finding a solution to his problem, but that was the way to gain knowledge—knowledge that would remain with him. Learning the multiplication facts could be accomplished faster by drill, but an appreciation of number relationships, though it would take longer to acquire by investigation, would result in more fundamental learning.

Fourth, the problem itself would discipline the child by holding him to his self-set task. No prizes, no false incentives, no standards imposed by adults would be used—or needed. And his learning would be interesting, challenging, and geared to his abilities.

Fifth, the teacher was to bear in mind that the child, not the subject matter, was the center of all teaching, his growth—mental, physical, and social—the objective of all endeavor. The teacher was expected to be aware of each child's ability to learn, of his strengths and limitations, and give these consideration in the daily planning. The teacher's task was thus to select really worthwhile experiences for the child, choosing problems which would arouse his curiosity, stimulate him to investigate, and challenge him to look at the world about him.

Over the preceding years, the school curriculum had become crowded with more and more factual material until the amount was staggering to both teacher and pupil. The teacher's problem, as Mr. Dewey saw it, was to make appropriate selections from this great body of facts, but always to be ready to alter or discard whatever experiences proved unchallenging. Teacher and pupil were to work together—questioning, investigating, planning. The teacher was to serve as a counselor, as a leader, and, when the child met a frustrating blockade, as a helper.

Furthermore, continuity was to be maintained so that the pupils would progress from a certain activity to a related one. In this way there would be no haphazard learning, and each pupil's previous experiences would be steppingstones to future ones.

There were other principles as well in Mr. Dewey's scheme of education, all deviating markedly from those followed in traditional schools.

Devoted teachers were needed to plan the Dewey School program and stand firm against the criticism that was bound to come from adherents of time-honored methods. To explain that every pupil would learn to read, write, and spell through an interest in literature and history, to explain that he would learn arithmetic as he needed to learn it for measurements in cooking, sewing, weaving, and woodwork must have demanded dedication and staunch belief in Mr. Dewey's ideas. The teachers' explanations met with incredulity. Allow the pupils freedom to move around the room, to investigate and talk with one another about their investigations, to get help from one another as well as give help? It was almost unthinkable. No competition? No prizes for giving back to the teacher what he had given them? No memorizing? No rote learning? No discipline except as it was imposed by problems? Even with Colonel Parker's work at Cook County Normal as a precedent, it took courage to stand up to the criticism, misunderstanding, and often ridicule that were directed at the Dewey School.

One can only admire those early teachers who were willing to devise, to investigate, to discard if necessary, to defend what they were doing—defend the freedom of the school, the new approach to reading, writing, and arithmetic, the lack of quiet and passivity, and the kind of discipline which the school stood for. Their guide-posts were Mr. Dewey's theories and principles, and their success lay in their dedication to childhood and happy learning.

THE PARENTS' ASSOCIATION

It was not only the teachers who needed to defend what they were doing. Parents, too, had to have reasons for sending their children to Mr. Dewey's unusual school, and they were often called on to justify the unorthodox activities carried on there.

During the school's first year, Mr. Dewey invited the parents to come together to discuss the questions raised about the school, to inform themselves and be able to answer critics. What they learned made them able to give sound psychological answers, though a more con-vincing argument was simply that the children greatly enjoyed going to the school, were learning, and were happy in doing so. Evidence that the parents were loyal supporters came at the end of the first half year, when there was a serious lack of funds. A staunch patron con-tributed $2,500, so that the school would be able to carry on.

At the beginning of the second year the Parents' Asso-ciation was formed. It had a double purpose: to assure financial support for the school and to provide information about its radical departures in method and content. The school enrollment was growing, and the new parents wanted to be informed.

The Parents' Association was, and still is, unique. It was called into being by the parents themselves and was first and foremost an instrument of education. Moreover, it was purely an organization of parents, not a parent-teacher association; in fact, the teachers were honorary, rather than regular, members. For three consecutive years a parents' class was formed, open to all members, in which Mr. Dewey set forth his theories, discussed them, and answered questions regarding the activities of the school. His book *School and Society* contains the lectures he gave before the Parents' Association.

While the basic aims of the association have changed somewhat with the years, it has never lost sight of its reason for being and has always continued to be an important adjunct, if not an integral part, of the school. It has widened its scope, greatly increased its membership, and maintained both its vigor and its unique quality.

THE NEIGHBORHOOD

Something should be said about the kind of neighborhood that would accept, foster, and support so unusual a school. Because of the nearby University, a goodly number of cultured, educated people lived in the Hyde Park–Kenwood area, which was known as a neighborhood of outstanding prestige. Doctors, bankers, lawyers, industrialists, as well as University men and women, had homes there—some palatial, some modest.

The Beginnings

The University, or perhaps its president, William Rainey Harper, attracted many persons who were leaders in their fields. They shared a spirit of inquiry and provided one another with stimulation and encouragement to explore new fields.

Many social changes that are now taken for granted were being discussed and promoted at the turn of the century: naturalization laws, prison reform, abolition of sweatshops, pure food laws, reduction of the twelve-hour working day, woman suffrage. The Columbian Exposition of 1893, held in Jackson Park and along the Midway, had not only demonstrated such new developments as electric power and light, but presented many new and thought-provoking ideas. Perhaps the outsider heard more about the Ferris wheel and the dances of Little Egypt at the Exposition than about the world congresses of religions and the new social ideas expressed there, but it was the latter which left a lasting imprint on the thinking of the time. In a neighborhood permeated by this atmosphere it was to be expected that the Dewey School would grow and flourish.

Two

The New School Thrives
1896–1900

Though the school had only "about twelve pupils" when it began in January, 1896, by October thirty-two pupils were enrolled, ranging in age from six to twelve. There were two full-time teachers—one in science (nature study) and one in history and literature—an instructor in manual training, a part-time instructor in music, and three graduate students as assistants.

Even before the end of its first year, the school had outgrown its original quarters. During Christmas vacation, 1896, it was moved to the South Park Club House on the southeast corner of Fifty-seventh Street and Rosalie Court (now Harper Avenue). Moving costs were paid by several loyal parents. New and larger quarters meant that more pupils could be admitted, and about a dozen were accepted out of the many who applied. Now more teachers were needed—and more money for their salaries.

Money, in fact, was always a problem. Tuition fees were low; in the beginning they were set at $12 a quarter, then later gradually raised to $25 a quarter for the older children. So contributions were sought and gratefully accepted. In the early years, the aggregate amounts given ranged from $3,000 to $5,000 a year. In 1899, individual contributions varied from $10 to $2,400.

By October, 1897, the enrollment was sixty, the teachers numbered sixteen, and the space was again inadequate. Again there was a quest for larger quarters, and a year later the school was moved to a large dwelling at 5412 Ellis Avenue. A barn, connected with the house by a covered way, was used for a gymnasium and manual training rooms.

From the start Mr. Dewey had hoped to include four- and five-year-old children in his school, but there was never quite enough money until, in 1898, the Castle family of Hawaii gave $1,500 for this special purpose. Thus the kindergarten was added and the age range extended. By the autumn of 1898, there were twenty children under six years of age among a total enrollment of ninety-five. The teaching staff had been increased to twelve full-time and seven part-time teachers. The latter were University students who were given free tuition in return for their services. The school remained at 5412 Ellis Avenue until 1903, when it moved into Emmons Blaine Hall.

TEACHERS AND CURRICULUM

When Mr. Dewey reported to President Harper on the year's work for 1897–98, he gave the total expenses for the year as $12,870, of which the major part, $9,160, went for teachers' salaries. Mr. Dewey explained that he had to pay good salaries in order to get good teachers. Many of his teachers, he added, could have commanded higher salaries elsewhere but chose to work with him because of their interest in the school.

In the beginning years of the school, Mr. Dewey

planned to keep children of different ages together, the older ones helping the younger, as in a family; but this idea was soon discarded. He had also wanted each group to be taught all subjects by one teacher but soon realized that if the work was to be challenging, stimulating, and thought provoking it should be done by specialists. By 1898, the school was on a departmental basis, and there were teacher specialists in literature, history, woodworking, science, physical education, textiles, cooking, and music.

The teacher's job was to introduce the children to a problem, then help them determine what could be done to solve it. He had to anticipate some of the more puzzling difficulties that might arise, help the pupils by questions and suggestions when they reached a blank wall, supply materials which they were not able to find, and give a hand whenever a pupil's ambitious plans were frustrated by his own limitations.

All the groups learned history, which Mr. Dewey viewed as a way of giving children "insight into social life." What was called science was largely nature study —observation of the world about them. The subject matter in history and science was left to the teacher to choose, organize for continuity, evaluate, and keep or discard.

The activities of the school, the experimentation that went on, and the laboratory aspects of the children's learning were of great interest to supporters and critics alike. Beginning in November, 1896, and continuing through the school year to June, 1897, the *University Record,* a small leaflet-type newspaper issued each Friday by the University, almost always contained a report on the work of some group in the Dewey School. The reports were presented in considerable detail so that

A graphic arts class sets type in a group project. School Calendars — monthly publications with school news and advertisements — were produced by high school students in the print shop.

parents, other teachers, and the University faculty would know precisely what was being done. From these reports, the following activities have been selected at random:

One of the younger groups cooked cereal, corn-meal, hominy, cranberry sauce, applesauce, cran-berry jelly, and stewed pears, apricots, and prunes. They weighed the sugar in ounces, measured other ingredients in cups, worked with fractions and other number facts, and learned to read the clock. Another activity, also in cooking, was a comparison of flaked, rolled, and cracked wheat with whole-grain wheat to discover how much starch each con-tained and hence the amount of water needed and the time required for cooking.

Group III, aged six and seven, boiled sugarcane to make syrup, separated cotton lint from the cot-tonseed, and dyed cotton cloth.

Group IV, aged seven and a half to eight, poured melted lead pipe into sand molds to make weights for scales, estimating the amount of lead to be melted for each weight. They also constructed thermometers.

Group V, aged eight to ten, looked at raw wool through a microscope, compared wool fibers with cotton fibers, carded wool by hand, and made a set of quilting frames in manual training class.

Group VI, the nine-year-olds, made pewter by fusing zinc, lead, and tin, adding bismuth, copper, and antimony.

Group VII, aged ten, planted seeds and experi-mented with the effects of different amounts of heat and moisture on germination.

The New School Thrives

Group VIII, eleven-year-olds, worked out a machine to straighten wool fibers.

Group IX, aged twelve, constructed a trefoil geometrically for one of the younger groups who needed it to make wood dies for printing cloth.

Group X, aged thirteen, took observations of the sun's altitude and used their findings to determine the latitude of Chicago.

The pupils were not divided into grades. The work was graded for continuity, but the children were grouped "on the basis of community interests, general intellectual capacity and mental alertness, and ability to do certain kinds of work." (*School and Society*, page 126.) Among the younger children, there were eight to ten in a group; among the older children, twelve to fifteen. There is no statement to indicate who did the grouping, but probably it was done by the teachers, working in close cooperation. Since this was before the day of intelligence and achievement testing, the teachers' observations must have served as criteria. There were no examinations, and no marks were given.

During the month of February, 1897, a day-by-day account of the work was presented in consecutive numbers of the *University Record*. Group IV, on a certain day, "spent thirty minutes in shop labelling their benches and working on new drafting boards, thirty minutes in quiet reading, thirty minutes in sewing, and an hour in preparing and serving luncheon which consisted of pea soup, boiled rice, and cocoa. In the afternoon, they read aloud Chapter X in Church's *Iliad*, stopping for discussion on points of special interest."

On the following Friday, the same group spent thirty minutes in shop, thirty minutes modeling the mountains and river valleys of Greece, guided by a blackboard map, and forty-five minutes in the gymnasium. When they returned in the afternoon, they wrote about what the Greeks thought of their gods, then read and discussed their papers.

FOREIGN LANGUAGES

Foreign languages were introduced to the children early. The teaching of French was begun in 1897 and was correlated with other subjects. Just as the learning of English grammar was incidental to other activities, so was French grammar. Conversation was paramount. The children learned to speak in French about their cooking, sewing, weaving, and shopwork. They learned French rhymes, sang French songs, dramatized French stories and folk legends, and talked with one another in French. This was a complete departure from the way languages were ordinarily taught at that time.

Two years later, in 1899, German and Latin were added and were also taught by the conversational method. French and German songs and plays appear in written records of the Christmas programs presented by the children. The history and literature of France and Germany were also included in this rich, interesting language curriculum.

THE HEALTH PROGRAM

The Dewey School health program was unique for its time. Early in the school's history a medical doctor was added to the faculty—a quite uncommon practice. Each child was given a personal physical examination in connection with the gymnasium program, and careful observations were made of his eyes, nose, throat, ears, heart, and lungs. Any defects were reported to the parents in order that the child could have corrective attention. Good posture was stressed. Tests were made for spinal curvatures, and twice a year measurements were taken for the correct adjustment of seats and desks.

The physical education program included outdoor play and games, whenever weather permitted, as well as indoor games and exercises. Wands and dumbbells, part of the gymnasium equipment, were effectively used in rhythms and dances. Not only were there play periods in the daily program but also playtime after school.

The health and physical activities program has, of course, changed over the years, but it has always been an important part of the scheme of the school.

FIELD TRIPS

Field trips were frequent—another unusual aspect of the curriculum. During 1896–97, an hour and a half was set aside on Monday mornings for trips to the Field Columbian Museum. This building, constructed for the 1893 Columbian Exposition, was located where the Museum of Science and Industry now stands and had a great variety of exhibits. The younger children had a plot of ground on the Wooded Island in Jackson Park where they often went to observe seasonal changes in nature. Older children went to the University laboratories to see such instruments as the interferometer and spectroscope. There were also longer trips—to the quarry on Stony Island where glacial markings were observed, to the cotton mills in Aurora to see the spinning of cotton, and others to Ravinia to see the clay bluffs, to Miller Station to see the sand dunes and desert, and to Sixty-third Street and the city limits to see a typical prairie area.

Some of the parents criticized the field trips as being too tiring and time consuming, but the trips remained an integral part of the school curriculum. Why learn from books what could better be learned through actual experience and observation?

VISITORS

Visitors came in numbers to see what was often called "the play school." They brought with them the concept of the accepted school of the day, described by Flora J. Cooke, principal of the Francis Parker School, in a paper read before the Parents' Association of that school on December 6, 1910:

> A few years ago in a great school in New York, I watched children take out their books, open them, and begin to study at the count of "One, two, three." They lifted their slates, poured on water, erased their work, again to count; they marched to place, stood in line, took position, read, spelled, or repeated the multiplication table and returned to seats. All worked as smoothly as a high power machine and it was the proud boast of the supervisor that she could go into any schoolroom of a given grade at a given hour and find the children working upon exactly the same lesson, using the same methods. This statement is not exaggerated.

With the above picture in mind, is it any wonder that visitors who found pupils moving about the room, conversing with one another, asking questions of the teacher instead of being asked, and following their interests,

34

The University of Chicago's campus facilities have always been available to the students at the Laboratory Schools. Here children work together on a project in the university Quadrangle. The observatory was recently moved to the top of the physics building, but elementary school classes are still welcome to use it.

thought the school was a place of laxness and disorder—
"a riot of uncontrolled liberty"? Some said that the
teachers in the Dewey School simply tried to amuse the
children by finding out what the pupils wanted to do
and then letting them do it. Others, however, saw the
value of the new method.

From the beginning, so many visitors came that someone had to be delegated to show them about and explain
the work, and by November, 1897, Mr. Dewey regretted
that there were not enough guides available. Visitors
were free to go from room to room—in fact, were invited by Mr. Dewey to make themselves at home—and
each room had extra chairs for them. In 1899, Mondays,
Tuesdays, and Thursdays were visiting days, and in the
next year, Mondays, Wednesdays, and Fridays were so
designated. Even today the school receives some two
thousand visitors a year.

A NEW NAME

In 1900, when the Dewey School was four years old, it
was referred to as the University Elementary School.
Some time afterward it began to be called the Laboratory School, harking back to Mr. Dewey's concept of it.
Ella Flagg Young, who in 1900 was associate professor
in the Department of Pedagogy and general supervisor
of instruction with Mr. Dewey, has been credited with
suggesting the name.

COMMUNICATION AND INTERCOMMUNICATION

An unusual system of communication was made necessary by the experimental nature of the school. During

the first years, when the teachers were attempting to find their way and were experimenting in different groups, weekly teachers' meetings were held. Here the work of the previous week was reported so that the teachers knew what was being done in all groups and with what success. They learned from one another as they exchanged views on problems, materials, and techniques. Also, teachers were given time to visit one another's groups and familiarize themselves with the over-all plan and operation of the school. Besides the informal teachers' meetings, there were formal seminar groups and pedagogical club meetings.

Pupils, too, knew about the activities of groups other than their own. At weekly assemblies different groups reported on projects, on trips taken or excursions made; they read stories they had written, gave plays they had authored, or sang songs they had composed. There were almost no long-rehearsed, formal programs. The presentations were kept free and natural, representing the children's own expressions. In addition, a school paper was printed weekly. Its production was supervised by one of the older groups, but younger groups contributed reports, stories, poems, and songs.

The Parents' Association was another vital means of communication. Not only did its members have Mr. Dewey's lectures to inform them, but they themselves brought up questions. The once-a-month meetings were supplemented by informal discussions, and the Dewey School was frequently the subject of spirited conversation at social events.

Add to the above the reports printed in the weekly *University Record,* and a more effective system of communication between parents, administrative staff, teachers, and pupils is difficult to imagine. As a result, each of them was personally concerned—and involved—with all that went on in the school.

By 1900, when the school had been in operation only four years, it was already known far and wide. The *University Record* reported this comment made at a meeting of the National Council of Education by Dr. A. B. Hinsdale of the University of Michigan: "More eyes are now fixed upon the University Elementary School at Chicago than upon any other elementary school in the country and probably in the world."

Well known, yes, but always in need of funds and always dependent, for its very survival, on the contributions of loyal parents and friends.

Three

Growth, Change, Challenge

1900—1904

COLONEL PARKER COMES TO THE UNIVERSITY

During Colonel Parker's eighteen years as head of the Cook County Normal School, he was continually beset by hostile politicians, who interfered with his work and hindered it, and by strongly conservative teachers and principals. In January, 1896, Cook County Normal was taken over by the city of Chicago. Renamed the Chicago City Normal School, it was controlled by the Cook County Commission, the majority of whose members were opposed to Colonel Parker's ideas.

In the two years which followed, there was such strong disagreement that it was almost impossible for Colonel Parker to continue to train teachers as he wished. At this juncture, Mrs. Emmons Blaine, whose son had been in the practice school and who was very much interested in Colonel Parker's work, realized that it was a serious waste of time for him to try to convince the Commission of the value of his plan of education. A wealthy woman, the daughter of Cyrus McCormick, inventor of the reaper, she offered Colonel Parker a million dollars, in money and property, to finance an independent school where he would be free to carry out his ideas. He accepted the offer, and in June, 1899, he and most of his faculty resigned from the City Normal. Since a new building had to be constructed for the private school, members of the faculty who resigned with him were given a year's leave, with salary, to study or to travel abroad.

In the following year, 1900, the architect's plans for the new school, to be known as the Chicago Institute, were ready. At this point, President Harper stepped in with another proposal: Would Colonel Parker bring his school to the University to form its School of Education?

After receiving President Harper's invitation, Colonel Parker did as he had always done with questions involving his school: he took it to his faculty. Some of his teachers were afraid of the proposal, afraid that their experimental work would again be hampered, this time by the University itself. But President Harper, on learning of their fears, wrote Colonel Parker in February, 1901, assuring him not only freedom to carry on his work but cooperation and help from the various departments of the University.

There was more discussion among Colonel Parker's faculty. Eventually it centered on one question: Where would Mrs. Blaine's generous gift do the most good? Finally, almost all the faculty voted to go with Colonel Parker to the University, even if they had to take cuts in salary.

Considerable correspondence was carried on between Colonel Parker and President Harper and between the president and Mrs. Blaine, since her gift would go with Colonel Parker to the School of Education. She stipulated that Colonel Parker be made director of the ele-

This old kiln in the basement of Blaine Hall was used to fire the treasures of many art students in the elementary and high schools. It has been replaced by smaller and more modern kilns located in the industrial arts areas.

mentary school and Mr. Dewey head of the high school department and that the School of Education include a pedagogic school, an elementary school, and a kindergarten. Mrs. Blaine's stipulations were met, and final agreements were reached early in March, 1901.

THE PARENTS PROTEST

These negotiations, however, were carried on without the knowledge of the Dewey School parents. Consequently, the announcement made at the Spring Convocation on March 19, 1901, that the Chicago Institute was to be affiliated with the University and that Colonel Parker would be director of the elementary school was like a bomb dropped in their midst.

The parents, greatly shocked, were fearful that their school, always in need of funds, would be swallowed up by the larger, wealthier institution and thus lose not only its distinctive identity but the progress made through its experimental techniques. Also, they objected to a training school; they did not want their children "practiced upon." They had great faith in Mr. Dewey and were opposed to the administration's relegating him to the high school headship.

A Parents' Association meeting was held forthwith—in the evening so that all members could attend. Here it was decided to ask the University Board of Trustees for permission to continue the Dewey School, provided the parents could assure the University of $5,000 a year in contributions. The trustees agreed, and a proposed budget and list of subscribers were submitted. The Dewey School, then, was to continue. The University would therefore have two elementary schools—one, a practice school for training teachers, under Colonel Parker, and a laboratory of the Department of Pedagogy, under Mr. Dewey.

Arrangements were made for a new building for the Chicago Institute, or the School of Education, to be erected at the corner of Fifty-eighth Street and Ellis Avenue (the present bookstore) at a cost of $25,000.

In July, 1901, Colonel Parker and his staff opened a summer session in Kozminski Public School. A student in his class that summer stated in a letter:

> I had a class with Colonel Parker in the Kozminski School. Often I have said his lectures changed completely my teaching career. He'd hold his dear, broad, fat hands out in gesture and tears would slip down as he would plead with us for consecration to teaching—especially for understanding the children.

In October, Colonel Parker and his faculty moved into the not-quite-finished new quarters, with 104 pupils and 28 faculty members. One of the teachers vividly recalled teaching music to the accompaniment of hammering, sawing, and planing.

Earlier, when plans were being made to build the Chicago Institute on Chicago's Near North Side, a branch school was begun on Webster Avenue to take care of the pupils who were registered for the school as it was originally planned. Mrs. Blaine gave the money for building the branch, and Flora J. Cooke, who had taught under Colonel Parker at Cook County and at Chicago Normal, was chosen as principal. The faculty was composed largely of teachers who had been trained under Colonel Parker. This was the beginning of the present Francis Parker School. Thus for a short time

The History of the Laboratory Schools

Colonel Parker was head of the North Side school named in his honor and of the South Side school on the University of Chicago campus.

SCAMMON COURT

The Chicago Institute, or School of Education, building was temporary. By 1901, plans were already fairly well formed for a new and larger one, known today as Emmons Blaine Hall, between Kimbark and Kenwood avenues.

Ground for the new building was made available by the widow of John Young Scammon. Mr. Scammon had been a trustee of the University, one of the founders of the Chicago Art Institute, an influential member of the Chicago Historical Society, a public-spirited citizen of Chicago, and a liberal friend of education. He had bought a large estate in the Fernwood addition to Hyde Park and had built a home on Fifty-eighth Street between Monroe (Kenwood) and Madison (Dorchester) avenues. Mrs. Scammon offered to sell "lots 5 to 16 in Block 2 in Fernwood addition to Hyde Park" to the University at half their valuation, on condition that the land be used solely and exclusively for University purposes and that it be called Scammon Court, in memory of her husband. The plaque bearing that name is on Emmons Blaine Hall in the southwest corner of the court, but the court is now commonly called Blaine Court; Mr. Scammon's name is perpetuated in Scammon Garden.

Growth, Change, Challenge

BLAINE HALL

Ground for the new building was broken in June, 1901, with appropriate ceremonies. The building was later named Emmons Blaine Hall in honor of Mrs. Blaine's deceased husband. On June 13, President Harper invited Mrs. Blaine to come to his house, "so that you may go in a carriage at ten minutes before twelve with Mr. and Mrs. Rockefeller and Professor Salisbury to Kent Theatre where the address by Professor Butler will be given.

"After these exercises the carriage will be driven to Scammon Court where the ground will be turned."

The *University Record* of June 28, 1901, reported that

> . . . a procession was formed to march to Scammon Court. At a stand erected in the Court, simple exercises were held. President Harper made a brief introductory statement. Colonel Parker then broke the ground for the new building and delivered an address ending with a quotation from Froebel: "Come let us live with the children."

It was well that Colonel Parker could turn the first shovel of earth, since he did not live to see the building completed. In the autumn of 1901, he was taken ill and went south to spend the winter in a warmer climate. In March, 1902, he died.

Two months after the death of Colonel Parker, Mr. Dewey was made director of the School of Education. Wilbur Samuel Jackman, a member of Colonel Parker's faculty, was appointed dean, and Mrs. Alice Dewey principal of the elementary school. The two schools continued in their separate establishments until October, 1903, when Emmons Blaine Hall was completed.

In the early 1900's, there was an organization known as the Francis W. Parker Club of Chicago, made up of teachers in the city schools who were friends and admirers of the great educator. This group commissioned a sculptor to make a bust of Colonel Parker, and on December 9, 1916, the bust was unveiled, presented to the University, and placed over the fireplace in Blaine Hall. Arthur J. Mason, who presented the gift and spoke for the donors, stated:

> The sculptor has placed the bust slightly turned to the entrance as though viewing, encouraging, welcoming the streams of earnest young people coming from all over the country, to acquire the ideas and ideals he strove so vigorously to establish.

The architecture of Blaine Hall was far ahead of that of most schools of the time. Classrooms were lighted by large windows on the south side of the building, and the many windows on the north side provided light for the corridors. As the architect, James Gamble Rogers, reported in the *University Record* (November, 1903):

> . . . it gives that which probably no school of its size in the world can be favored with—namely, sunlight in every classroom at some time of the day.

Quoting further from his report:

> One quite noteworthy feature in the plan of this building is the concrete floor construction. A cement slab 25 by 88 is an immense piece of cement. There are in the School of Education [Blaine Hall] twelve such slabs. . . . These slabs were tested in a practical manner.

The method of the test was to fill a room full of bricks. . . . But as the floor showed no effects whatever from the test, two iron beams were placed in the middle of the span of the room, and on these the whole load of a room full of bricks was concentrated. Not only was there no breakage, but there was no appreciable deflection of the floor.

The building reflected Colonel Parker's philosophy. Its rooms were designed for many activities. In full-size and half-size grade rooms special activities correlated with the subject matter could be carried on. There were casting and kiln rooms, home economics and shop rooms, dyeing and textile rooms, a library, and a museum—all uncommon for their time. Over the years, these rooms have lent themselves admirably to the changing needs and expansion of the school.

FACTIONS AND FRICTION

In its first three months, Emmons Blaine Hall housed Mr. Dewey's school, Colonel Parker's elementary school and kindergarten, the School of Education, and the manual training school. (The last named was moved to Belfield Hall in January, 1904.) In 1903, the two elementary schools were brought together under one roof, and the process of welding the two units into one went on slowly, laboriously, and not always amicably. There were cliques and antagonisms. The Dewey teachers were devoted to Mr. Dewey, and the Parker teachers equally devoted to Colonel Parker's ideas. The latter group had Mrs. Blaine as an ally, and whenever there were difficulties, she would write President Harper, asking him to have the troublesome matters settled. There was a

47

A fifth-grade class learns French words and phrases relating to food as they enjoy lunch together. This is an example of easy memorization through meaningful and interesting activities, as advocated in Dewey's early plans. Foreign language classes have long been a part of the Laboratory Schools curriculum.

strained relationship between Mr. Dewey and the Parker teachers. When Mrs. Blaine was not writing President Harper, Mr. Jackman was. Some of his complaints were that Mr. Dewey did not include the Parker teachers on committees and in conferences, that faculty meetings were not called regularly, that Mr. Dewey's attitude was a "philosophic one—coldly scientific," and that he absented himself from important meetings. Mr. Jackman evidently felt that the Parker group was being frozen out, for he wrote President Harper that "the glacial epoch should be brought to speedy termination." Further, Mrs. Dewey was unacceptable as principal of the elementary school, especially to the Parker teachers.

Early in 1904, Mr. Dewey was told that Mrs. Dewey's position would terminate at the close of the year. Shortly thereafter, he himself resigned, though he requested President Harper to make it clear to the Board of Trustees that his reason for resigning was not the president's refusal to reappoint Mrs. Dewey. The real reason, as given by Mr. Dewey's daughters in a later book, was President Harper's indifference and hostility to the Dewey School. The resignation took effect January 1, 1905, but Mr. Dewey's active connection with the University ceased at the close of spring quarter in 1904.

PASSING OF THE PIONEERS

Colonel Parker was dead. Mr. Dewey had resigned. Seemingly the Laboratory School, the school of experimentation, had ceased to be—but only seemingly. The school has changed, to be sure, but the influence of the two men has never been eradicated. They put their indelible stamp on the school, and much of their basic philosophy has remained.

Freedom for both children and teachers has ever been the key word at the school—not undisciplined but purposeful freedom. The idea that children need freedom to investigate, to experiment, to move about, to exchange ideas, and to challenge has never been lost. Truly it can be said that there are few children in the United States whose school experiences have not been made more meaningful and enjoyable because of the ideas and philosophy of John Dewey and Francis Parker.

THE UNIVERSITY HIGH SCHOOL

The University of Chicago High School was composed of several schools: the Chicago Manual Training School, the South Side Academy, and the University Laboratory School. The Chicago Manual Training School had an endowment fund of $50,000 given by John Crerar, a large but rather poor building, and a valuable piece of property which was later sold for $200,000. In 1897, the school was united with the University of Chicago, and President Harper became its official head, though it remained at its Twelfth and Michigan location.

The other large school which came to be a part of University High School was the South Side Academy, founded in 1892 by E. O. Sissoon, a former teacher in the Morgan Park Academy of the University of Chicago. In 1897, William Bishop Owen succeeded Mr. Sissoon as dean, and in 1899, the school moved into a new home at 5467 Lexington Avenue, which was large enough to accommodate two hundred students.

By 1901, the older pupils who had enrolled at the Dewey School during its first years were in high school. They formed the third school which joined with the Chicago Manual Training School and the South Side Academy to become the University High School. In

Growth, Change, Challenge

July, 1901, Mr. Dewey began his work as director of the University Secondary School. Mr. Owen continued as dean of the South Side Academy, and Mr. Belfield as dean of the Chicago Manual Training School.

There was no central building for the three schools, and not until January, 1904, did they come together under one roof. In June, 1902, ground was broken for the new building, then called the Manual Training Building and now known as Henry Holmes Belfield Hall. The cornerstone was laid a year later, with a mallet and trowel made by the Manual Training students.

The new name, University High School, was arrived at after considerable discussion. The statement of its adoption included a qualification: "it being understood that the Chicago Manual Training School constitute the technological course, . . . and as such, it has its own dean, course of study, circulars . . ."

In the summer of 1903, most of the Manual Training School machinery and other equipment was moved from Twelfth and Michigan to the University, where it was stored awaiting completion of the new building. From October, 1903, to January, 1904, academic and shop work were carried on in the newly completed Blaine Hall, but in January, 1904, the shop work was transferred to the new Manual Training Building.

The existence of two heads of the University High School, Mr. Owen and Mr. Belfield, was an indication of the difficulties in forming one school out of three. The student bodies of the two larger schools were strongly antagonistic, and the prediction was made that it would be impossible to get rid of this partisan feeling. Each school had its own traditions, its loyal students and alumni, its patrons. In the fall of 1904, however, unity was achieved, suddenly and completely, through a non-academic demonstration of superiority: The University High School had the best football team of all the preparatory schools in Chicago.

In its first year the high school had an enrollment of 552—123 students from the Manual Training School, 125 from the South Side Academy, 41 from the Laboratory School, and the remainder from the central and western parts of the United States. Its reputation for scholastic excellence was known far and wide, and its manual training school ranked with those in St. Louis and Baltimore as the first in America.

Despite the fact that the high school and the elementary school were located in the same city block, and but a stone's throw from one another, they operated as distinctly separate institutions. The elementary school had been from its inception an experimental school, used by professional educators as a laboratory; the high school concentrated on instructing its students. At the same time, University High was not a trade school. Its purpose was not to make things, even though one of its components was the Manual Training School. According to Mr. Belfield, the school stood for accuracy of thought, honesty of work, clear thinking, and the development of judgment and will power.

It was not long, however, before a laboratory aspect began to be evident in the high school. Two problems came under investigation: One was the revision of the mathematics curriculum, with the innovation of correlating learning experiences in algebra and geometry. The other was the coordination of the social organization of the school, so that the students' social life there would be truly educative. Fraternities and sororities were abolished, and clubs, social and scholastic, were established within the school.

Four

Five Fruitful Years

1904—1909

THE ELEMENTARY SCHOOL CARRIES ON

Six teachers who had taught under Mr. Dewey stayed on in the elementary school. One of them, Harry Orrin Gillet, was identified with the school for the next thirty-eight years. Except for this small group and some new additions, the faculty was composed of teachers who had taught under Colonel Parker. After Mr. Dewey's resignation, Wilbur Samuel Jackman, who had been dean of the College of Education, was made principal of the elementary school. No director was appointed, and the position remained unfilled until 1909.

Mr. Jackman had come to the Cook County Normal School in 1889 to take over the department of natural sciences. Colonel Parker depended on his help and counsel in all administrative matters. The two had similar ideas on education and worked together admirably, each respecting and admiring the other.

Mr. Jackman was an able organizer and something of an autocrat, yet he believed every teacher should be free to work out his problems within the framework that had been established by the faculty. In view of Mr. Jackman's organizing abilities, it is easy to see how he

53

On the fourth floor of Blaine Hall, beneath the natural light from the skylights, children learn to prepare wool for the looms.

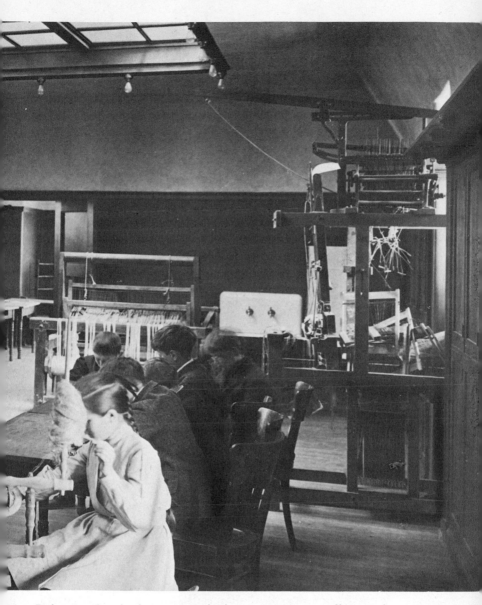

Dying wool, spinning, and designing patterns were all part of the elementary school art program.

and Mr. Dewey must have irked one another during the time they worked together under one roof.

Mr. Jackman had an exceptionally keen mind, a very fluent pen, and seemingly limitless energy. A prolific writer, in the seven years between 1891 and 1898, while he was at Cook County Normal, he wrote six books on the teaching of nature study. In an article in *Science Teacher* for February, 1957, Gerald S. Craig called Mr. Jackman the father of modern elementary science. Other writers have said that Mr. Jackman's experimentation was not *on* children but *with* children and that he never lost sight of the child's interests and capabilities. He was an able guide in the science movement, since he was not only a specialist in the field but also an experienced teacher. In 1904, he was the author of the Third Yearbook of the National Society for Scientific Study of Education (later the National Society for the Study of Education), a book devoted to the problems of teaching science and the first yearbook of the Society devoted to the subject. He contributed to other educational publications as well.

When he became principal of the elementary school, Mr. Jackman also became editor of the *Elementary School Teacher*—an outgrowth of Colonel Parker's *Course of Study,* which contained material prepared by the teachers, with outlines, book references, and illustrations. With the exception of one or two issues, he wrote the editorials, all of them lengthy, from 1904 to 1907. He encouraged his teachers to write, and from time to time articles by them appeared in the *Elementary School Teacher*. As editor, he stated, he did not ask for perfectly prepared materials, but he wanted teachers, parents, and friends of the school informed on what was being attempted there.

Five Fruitful Years

School was dismissed every Monday afternoon to provide time for faculty meetings. Routine business was managed through committees, and the main part of the meetings was given over to discussions of educational principles involved in each teacher's work. Mr. Jackson once wrote that the purpose of such discussions was not to settle educational questions but to keep them everlastingly open, so that changes could be made as readily as possible.

The curriculum continued to be rich and varied. For example, the nine-to-ten-year-old group had nature study, applied science, geography, history, mathematics, reading, English—which included literature, dramatics, spelling, and writing—French, German, drawing and painting, modeling, woodworking, cooking, metalwork, textiles, music, and gymnastics. The field trips continued, and continued also to be criticized by some of the parents as too taxing for the children. In an editorial in the June, 1905, issue of the *Elementary School Teacher*, Mr. Jackman wrote:

> . . . it is simply ridiculous to keep children confined in a schoolroom learning *about* a world while they must live *in* it.

He further affirmed that trips and excursions would be retained as part of the curriculum.

At the April, 1905, Parents' Association meeting, the perennial problem of homework was brought up, with a request for some system of assigning it. Mr. Jackman remarked that he was continually being beset by parents who wanted their children to have more homework. What was done about this problem is not clear, but at a meeting a year later a parent referred to the question of homework as "a ghost which ever rose and would never be put down." The ghost still walks.

One infers that some parents may have put pressure on the administration to have their children advanced by grades. Grade levels were a bane to Mr. Jackman; in an editorial he called the school grade "a pure fiction in philosophy, but a stubborn and unreasonable fact in practice."

For the following year he outlined a plan of organization which would eliminate as far as possible the hard-and-fast lines that usually separate different grades, and would thus allow the pupils to advance through school without being impeded by grade structure. The term *grade* was to be banished, and divisions, sections, classes, and groups were to be set up to give each pupil an opportunity to work with whatever group his abilities best fitted. In this way he would have greater freedom to proceed at his own rate. The idea was good, but it did not materialize. The same problem has arisen many times since, and many solutions have been offered and tried, but grades and grade divisions persist.

Mr. Jackman came up with another suggestion designed to break down grade barriers. The plan was to form eighteen clubs among which the pupils could choose those they wished to work in. The clubs were diverse: civics, woodworking, gymnastics, metalworking, cooking, camera, field, dancing, sketching, dramatics, school paper, electricity, garden, toolhouse construction, textiles, clay modeling, microscope, bookbinding, and printing. Pupils of different ages worked together, and when Mr. Jackman, in June, 1906, evaluated the work of the preceding quarter, he commented on the value of the clubs. However, he stated also that a more effective plan of organization was needed. So grade divisions were continued, despite all attempts to eliminate them.

Since the school was set up for the training of teachers and since the critic teachers had to have curriculum content ready for the trainees, careful advance planning was necessary. This would seem to exclude creative work, but actually it did not. For instance, each group in the first six grades was encouraged to write, cooperatively, at least one complete original song. In French, German, literature, and history classes, there were dramatic productions, to which children, teachers, and assistants contributed. At Thanksgiving and Christmas, there were pageants and programs, sometimes including all the children in the school, for which much of the written material was prepared by the teachers, their assistants, and the pupils.

The school enrollment rose steadily. In 1906–7, during the autumn quarter, there were 405 pupils, with a waiting list of 70. Blaine Hall was taxed to capacity for space, since the School of Education occupied the same building.

In June, 1905, Mr. Jackman devoted the entire issue of the *Elementary School Teacher* to one article, "The University Elementary School, Its General Plan and Course of Study," written by himself. Here he formulated some of the school's guiding principles:

> The School realizes the utter futility of trying to teach anyone anything when he is not in a happy frame of mind.

> The value of the School and teaching is determined wholly by the quality of the life which it enables the pupil to live.

> The emphasis is not placed upon text books nor

upon subjects of study as ends. It is placed upon Quality of Life as this expresses itself in good taste, helpfulness, gentleness of spirit, sensitiveness of rights of others, initiative, fidelity to conviction and trustworthiness—all of which are so necessary in realization of democratic ideals.

On Monday morning, January 28, 1907, the entire University was shocked to hear of Mr. Jackman's death. He had had a cold the preceding week, but it had not kept him from his varied activities or from a social gathering with School of Education students on Saturday evening. By Sunday morning pneumonia had developed, and on Monday morning he died.

The Parents' Association commemorated Mr. Jackman's achievements in a most appropriate way. Already the association was planning to equip a playground on the property between Monroe (Kenwood) and Madison (Dorchester) avenues, fronting on the Midway—property which John D. Rockefeller, Sr., gave to the University in December, 1903. The Parents' Association named this playground Jackman Field. How fitting that the man who strove to advance nature study, who has been called the father of elementary science in the schools, should have a piece of the great out-of-doors dedicated to his memory!

After Mr. Jackman's death, the elementary school was conducted by an executive committee, the Committee on Management, appointed by the president of the University. Three teachers who had been connected with the school for several years—Harry Orrin Gillet, Zonia Baber, and Emily Rice—were members of this committee.

Mr. Gillet had come to the Dewey School in 1901 as

an assistant in teaching science. When Mr. Dewey resigned, Mr. Gillet was one of the six teachers who stayed on. Under Mr. Jackman, he was made assistant principal and taught eighth grade. In 1909, he was appointed principal, a position he held until he retired in 1944.

Zonia Baber was a graduate of the Cook County Normal School, where she had studied under Colonel Parker. She later taught under his direction in the Chicago Normal School and went with him from there to the School of Education. She served as principal in Colonel Parker's school in 1901–2. From 1902 to 1922, when she retired, she was associate professor in the School of Education, teaching geography and geology. Miss Baber was one of the founders of the Geographic Society of Chicago and a member of the Society of Woman Geographers. In the first suffragist parade in Washington, D.C., when Woodrow Wilson was inaugurated, she and Emily Rice were among the marchers.

Miss Rice had taught history and literature under Colonel Parker at Cook County Normal School and had gone with him to the School of Education. She was, according to one of her co workers, a delicate, attractive little person, a fine student of history, and one of the leaders in advanced educational thought.

It was Mr. Gillet who reported to the president on the work in the elementary school for 1907–8. The faculty, he wrote, had been divided into three groups to study (1) the organization of the school in its relation to the physical and social welfare of the children and (2) the desirability of further specialization in teaching. Each group had reported the results of its investigations at five weekly faculty meetings. As for the pupils, their accomplishments included improving the *Elementary School Reporter,* their own monthly magazine;

designing and selling a school calendar; writing and presenting a play, *Iliad*; and organized teaching in a printshop. (The sale of the calendar provided additional equipment for the shop.) Toward the close of the year, the school presented a series of exhibits for the parents, showing shop, laboratory, and gymnastic work.

Another report on the year's work was the "Course of Study of the University Elementary School" published in the May, 1908, issue of the *Elementary School Teacher*. Bertha Payne had taken over the editorship after Mr. Jackman's death, and the "Course of Study" was published as it had been in previous years. Some of the activities listed were (1) the museum, a display of pupils' handwork; (2) the Saturday field trips, which were open to students, parents, and teachers; (3) the monthly magazine, written and published by the children; (4) the school gardens, in which the pupils grew common vegetables, grains, household herbs, and miscellaneous plants such as hemp, sugar beets, tobacco, cotton, and peanuts. A new activity was mentioned: In the eighth grade formal grammar was begun as part of the printshop work.

The assemblies were continued, though the school at this time had so large an enrollment that not all the students could be accommodated in one assembly. Two assemblies were held each week for the lower grades (1–4) and two for the upper grades (5–8).

Interest in dramatics was high. French classes presented French plays, German classes presented German plays, and history and literature classes dramatized events and episodes from these fields. Teachers and pupils worked together on the plays, not only writing and producing them but cutting and sewing the costumes in the sewing room and dyeing them in dye vats.

The Black Knights and the White Knights in combat in Scam-mons Garden. The togas and helmets would indicate Greek warriors. The study of Greece and Rome are still a part of the fourth-grade curriculum.

Holidays were always celebrated by some kind of drama. At Thanksgiving, a procession of children, costumed in smocks of yellow, orange, brown, red, and green and bearing woven baskets of fruits and vegetables, marched through the corridors to the stage in Room 214, where the Thanksgiving program was held. At Christmas, there were French plays, French troubadours, German songs and plays, and English waits, and the Yule log and the boar's head were carried to the fireplace on the first floor. In the spring, there were plays and dances in Scammon Garden.

At about this time, the Parents' Association was reorganized. In each of the nine grades (which included the kindergarten) four mothers' meetings were held during the year. A chairman and a secretary from each room were elected at the beginning of the school year, and the nine grade chairmen and the Parents' Association chairman made up the Home and Education Committee. In the months when there were no separate grade meetings, all the mothers and teachers came together to hear and discuss a paper on some subject of mutual interest and to chat with one another informally.

Two projects in which parents and children cooperated were the establishment of an art fund, for the purpose of providing paintings and prints for the corridors and classrooms, and, in December, the construction of simple toys and presents for the Visiting Nurses Association.

While the working relationship between the School of Education, the Graduate Department of Education, and the elementary school had been close from the time of Colonel Parker, it appears to have been strengthened during the year 1908–9. The *Annual Register* noted that the School and the Department of Education were now participating in the formulation of the course of study and general plans for the conduct of the elementary school. Practice teachers were supervised by the grade teacher and by a member of the Graduate Education Department, who was responsible for the methods courses. Such a step was probably deemed necessary because the elementary school had had no director since Mr. Dewey's resignation.

THE UNIVERSITY HIGH SCHOOL—PROGRESS AND PROBLEMS

Just as in the elementary school, there were also several administrative changes in the high school. At the end of the year 1907-8, Mr. Belfield retired and William Bishop Owen was appointed dean, with Franklin W. Johnson as assistant dean. A little more than a year later, in November, 1909, Mr. Owen resigned to become principal of the Chicago Normal School, and Mr. Johnson was made principal of the high school. But these changes in administration seemed to make little difference in the school's purpose and progress. The terms of service of those in administrative posts overlapped, and the stability of the faculty made possible a continuity of experimentation as well as high standards in academic work.

In 1909, inspectors from the University of Illinois asked permission to visit the University High School, with the idea of placing the school on the accredited list of the North Central Association of Secondary Schools and Colleges. Permission was granted, the inspection was made, and in April, 1911, Mr. Johnson reported that the University High School had been placed on the North Central Association's accredited list.

The revision of the mathematics curriculum, begun in the earliest days of the school, continued. In fact, the mathematics department was far ahead of all other departments in the high school—in the number of articles written, the experimentation carried on, and the books published. The *School Review* for January, 1906, October, 1906, and October, 1907, carried influential articles on the teaching of mathematics in the high school —the result of the work of "a corps of zealous and admittedly successful practical teachers." In this same year, 1906–7, the *School Review* published more articles by the high school faculty than in any preceding year, articles on the teaching of science, history, and the classics as well as mathematics.

The high school had an unusual number of student publications. The *University High School Weekly* was begun in December, 1903. In March, 1907, the first daily paper was issued. At first called the *Daily Maroon and Black*, it soon became the *University High School Daily*, a four-page publication edited by a different group of students each day of the week. In 1908, the *Midway*, a monthly literary magazine, was launched, containing original contributions from students and selected class themes. The school's yearbook, the *Correlator*, made its initial appearance in 1904. The name *Correlator* was chosen because correlation was the underlying principle in the school's scheme of study. The yearbook continued to carry this name for the next forty years.

By 1909, then, University High School had a daily paper, a monthly literary magazine, and a yearbook. A great many students were involved in their production and represented in the contributions. Considering its size, the school's literary output was large indeed—and of high quality.

One problem faced by the school staff from the begin-ning was that of working out a truly educative social life for its students. As Mr. Owen wrote in the January, 1907, *School Review*: "The school is a social institution in that it is the means for socializing future members of society. . . . If a school brings children together, it should teach them to live . . . serious and useful, but also glad and happy lives."

The social life of the high school included dances in the temporary gymnasium on Friday afternoons during the autumn and winter quarters. The end of each quarter was marked by a special dance, for which the Parents' Association provided music, refreshments, and favors. In few schools in the United States was the students' social activity so well coordinated and a matter of such active concern to students, faculty, and parents.

The school's social life was not without its problems, however. A seemingly never ending one, from the very first year and for many years thereafter, was that of fraternities. Motions to ban them were made in faculty meetings. Articles were written for the *Elementary School Teacher* and the *School Review* decrying their existence. The Parents' Association was asked to help rid the school of them. Students were asked to sign a pledge not to join a fraternity or sorority, and several students were dismissed from school for violating the ban. But fraternities could not be suppressed entirely.

Members of the faculty felt that prohibiting fraterni-ties would accomplish little unless the students were offered something to replace them. Many ideas were suggested and explored, notably the formation of in-

To correlate mathematics with social studies, an intermediate class built sextants and attempted to "shoot" the sun to determine their latitude. Later intermediate students have also participated in this kind of experience.

terest clubs. In 1903–4, there were two literary societies, an orchestra, a mandolin club, a dancing class, and several cooking classes. In 1907, the organization of photography, crafts, German, and Latin clubs was recommended to augment the science and arts clubs already in existence. During the year 1907–8, the Press Club, the Blaine Club, and the camera, mandolin, sketch, U-Hi, and sophomore debating clubs were organized. In 1909, the engineering and dramatics clubs joined the list. Yet despite this great array of interest clubs, the fraternity problem was never completely solved.

The U-Hi Club got its own clubhouse in the spring of 1907, mainly because some students had been frequenting the poolrooms on Fifty-fifth Street. Since others thought that this was not in keeping with the standards the school hoped to maintain, five students came up with the idea for a clubhouse where boys could go after school for a game of billiards, pool, or cards. The five formed themselves into a committee, prepared a statement of their proposal, and presented it to the faculty, who endorsed it. The Parents' Association also promised support. A constitution and bylaws were drawn up, and shortly thereafter the trustees offered the house at 5835 Kimbark Avenue, between Blaine Hall and the Manual Training Building (now Belfield Hall), as a clubhouse.

Other organizations such as the Student Council and honor societies developed early. The Student Council was made up of representatives from each class, and the number varied from year to year. In 1909, there were fifteen members: the presidents of the four classes, four members from the senior class, three from the junior class, and two each from the sophomore and freshman classes. The purpose of the Council was to aid in the government of the school.

In April, 1905, the faculty was presented with a tentative plan for the organization of an honor society, to be made up of students who had been very useful in the life of the school. In 1908, a boys' honor society called the Tripple E was formed by the students themselves. (The reason for misspelling the word "triple" was not given.) In December, 1909, Mr. Johnson wrote of a group of honor societies:

> [They] . . . present what is perhaps a unique feature in the high school. One of these open to both boys and girls is based on scholarship. Its object is to maintain the standard of scholarship and promote good fellowship among members of the school.

Five

Testing, Testing, Testing
1909–1919

In the spring of 1909, Charles Hubbard Judd came to the University of Chicago as head of the Department of Education and director of the University Elementary School and the University High School. The two schools were still separate entities, and there was little overlapping between them. At last, however, they had a director after four directorless years.

Mr. Judd's specialties were psychology and pedagogy. Thus his professional background was similar to Mr. Dewey's, but his method of operation was quite different. A graduate of Wesleyan University in 1894, he had taken his doctorate under Wundt at the University of Leipzig in 1896. Between 1896 and 1902, he was professor of psychology and pedagogy, first at New York University and then at the University of Cincinnati. In 1902, he accepted an instructorship at Yale, and in 1904 was promoted to assistant professor. While at New Haven, he was also director of the psychological laboratory.

The portrait of him which hangs in the Judd Hall common room shows a man of vigor and forcefulness, a dominant, dynamic personality. Mr. Judd had a keen, analytical mind and a brilliant wit. He would tolerate little opposition, and those who had the temerity to disagree with him often found it expedient to seek another position.

Propelled by Mr. Judd at Chicago and William H. Kilpatrick at Columbia University, a new scientific movement in education got under way and gained momentum. Its key principle was "concerted analysis of the learning process under laboratory conditions." At Chicago, the elementary school was the chief laboratory of the movement, although some experimentation was carried on in the high school. Not only the faculty of the Department of Education but the students and also the teachers in the elementary school took part in the laboratory experiments. Elementary school pupils referred to themselves as guinea pigs, and well they might. They were used for research, experimentation, and refinement of tests by teachers, graduate students, and faculty. Tests were given so often that the pupils lost their fear of them; in fact, in some instances they took them far too lightly for the testers' satisfaction.

As soon as he arrived, Mr. Judd began writing the editorials in the *Elementary School Teacher*. In those editorials the following words and phrases appear repeatedly, testifying to his beliefs: "efficiency," "closer organization," "thoroughly organized course of study," "systematic, sequential work." The tightening of the reins, the guiding of the team, and the discarding of the trivial in every aspect of the school program—all these principles were revealed early, both in his writings and in his actions.

While Colonel Parker was director, there had been

a close relationship between the School of Education and the University Elementary School, inasmuch as the elementary school was a practice school and the School of Education gave the methods courses. During Mr. Judd's directorship, a very different relationship was established. Professors in the School of Education were made supervisors of subject areas in the elementary school and dealt directly with the teachers.

Three professors who came to the University at the same time as Mr. Judd were given responsibility for specific areas: Otis W. Caldwell, Walter Sargent, and Samuel Chester Parker. They were members of the Graduate Education Department as well as supervisors, and each was in charge not only of the teaching of a particular subject area but of the formulation of the course of study.

Mr. Caldwell was placed in charge of science, which was more frequently called nature study. He directed all science work, drew up the course of study, and supervised the teaching. In the *Elementary School Teacher,* from November, 1909, through October, 1910, Mr. Caldwell presented, in article form, a graded course of study, entitled "Nature Study in the Grades," which included elements of botany, zoology, physics, and chemistry. Not all the material was new, however; some of it had been drawn from outlines previously made by teachers in the grades.

Mr. Sargent, an artist as well as a teacher of art education, organized the work in art and manual training throughout the elementary school and supervised the teaching. His course of study was printed in the *Elementary School Teacher* in a series of articles entitled "The Fine and Industrial Arts in Elementary Schools."

The History of the Laboratory Schools

These articles by Mr. Caldwell and Mr. Sargent were influential in setting patterns for courses of study in both science and art in many of the nation's schools.

Mr. Parker was in charge of practice teaching as well as a member of the faculty in the Graduate Education Department.

The three professors reported to Mr. Judd, who in turn reported to the president, on all research, on books and articles written, and on experimentation in the schools. By 1912, the three, who had been named as successors to Mr. Jackman, were no longer so identified on the faculty list.

Other men in the Education Department were also active in experimentation, in research, and above all in the field of testing; in fact, the decade 1909–19 was marked by a fever of testing, not only in the university schools but across the nation. Mr. Judd was one of several educators who, through his prolific writing, his numerous addresses to educational groups, and his graduate students, spread the contagion. Standards of accomplishment which could be expected at various grade levels were determined by testing, and standardized tests came to occupy a prominent place among methods of supervision.

Among many educators who devised tests during this period were the faculty and the graduate students in the School of Education, and (as already noted) the elementary school children were given almost every one of these tests.

For example, for five years Frank Nugent Freeman carried on studies of handwriting. In one study he gathered statistical data from six elementary schools, including the University Elementary School. His theoretical aim was to analyze the handwriting of good and poor writers, and determine what made good handwriting good and poor handwriting poor. His practical aim was to find a way of helping pupils improve their handwriting. A graduate student worked out an experimental course of study with a group of about thirty children, ranging from second- to sixth-graders, all of whom needed special training in handwriting.

A number of studies of reading were also made, and these necessitated the use of standardized tests for purposes of comparison. William Scott Gray, one of the first educators to construct a standardized test to measure reading achievement, produced an oral reading test and used University Elementary School pupils to establish validity. Silent reading tests were also given the pupils, to determine how long the tests should be and to check the validity of two methods of scoring. Clarence Truman Gray, a graduate student, gave a number of reading comprehension tests to determine rate and quality of silent and oral reading.

Guy T. Buswell made a study of the eye-voice span in reading—that is, the distance by which the eye leads the voice in oral reading. Another student made a stenographic record of the first-grade reading class in order to investigate children's progress, their difficulties, remedial measures which the teacher applied, and the effectiveness of those measures. Then, too, case studies were made of five pupils who were considered the poorest readers in their respective classes. After being given standardized tests to diagnose reading difficulties, each pupil was taught individually to correct his reading deficiency.

Several studies were made by graduate students in an effort to find the best way to teach spelling. In one study, the children in grades four through eight were given preliminary spelling tests, then were taught to correct their misspellings by placing special emphasis on the difficult part of the word. Another study of poor spellers in grades four through seven of the elementary school tried to determine which of two methods of visual presentation was more efficient in teaching spelling.

Studies in arithmetic, science, and art were also made, using tests, tests, and more tests. The pupils in the Laboratory Schools of that era can never know the breadth and depth of their contributions to the science of education.

Of course the schools had been laboratories in Mr. Dewey's and Colonel Parker's time, but now the approach was quite different though the goal was the same: better teaching, improved learning, and increased interest on the part of the pupils. Take dramatics, for example. Both Mr. Dewey and Colonel Parker saw it as a vehicle for learning in many areas. Mr. Judd, however, was impatient with the amount of time the children spent in diverse activities, such as sewing and dyeing costumes as well as staging and organizing the production.

Did all this research and testing reveal the best way to teach reading, writing, spelling, arithmetic, and science? Not *the* best way, but many good ways. The testing era not only made teachers aware that there are several roads to learning, but it stimulated thought and investigation. The value of the standardized test was that it afforded a means of comparative measurement, and as such it was an excellent instrument. Like the intelligence test, it could also be misused, as when test scores were accepted without question or comparison.

Were the principles of Mr. Dewey and Colonel Parker

lost sight of in this period of emphasis on testing and on the scientific study of the learning process? Despite the scientific overlay, the teachers who had been trained under Mr. Dewey and Colonel Parker continued to follow the teachings of the two men. The hand as well as the head still had an important part in the children's learning.

A Seven-Year School. In his 1912–13 report to University of Chicago President Harry Pratt Judson, Mr. Judd was able to state that the experiment of reducing the elementary school from eight years to seven had been completed. This idea of shortening the period of elementary schooling by one year was not new. Actually, Mr. Dewey had proposed a six-year elementary school in an article in the *School Review* in January, 1903. He felt that the aim of elementary education— to develop an active interest in truth—ought to be accomplished in six years. By shortening the period, he wrote,

> . . . the elementary school child would be relieved of its two chief time-wasting factors: daily repetition of drill in rudiments which have previously been mastered; and anticipation of advance subject matter so difficult that it can be pursued intelligently only at a later period.

An article in the *Elementary School Teacher* for February, 1913, described how the eighth grade was successfully eliminated. A conference was called of the teachers of the seventh and eighth grades and the first year of high school. There each subject was explored to find out what was being taught and how far all subjects were interrelated. Then a course of study was set up, based on these findings.

At the end of the next year, 1913–14, Mr. Johnson wrote in his report to the president:

> . . . Judged by the results of the year's work, the elimination of the 8th grade has proved a complete success. The pupils promoted to the High School at the end of the 7th grade made a distinctly better record in each subject during the year than a larger number of pupils coming from schools requiring eight years.

"Spread the Gospel." Mr. Judd urged the teachers to write, and write they did. In September, 1914, the *Elementary School Teacher* became the *Elementary School Journal,* and with the change in name came a change in policy. For five years most of the articles had been devoted to problems of general organization and had been written not by classroom teachers, as they had under Colonel Parker and Mr. Jackman, but by faculty members of the University or by the administrative staff. Now the *Journal* was enlarged, and classroom teachers again contributed. Among their articles were courses of study which had been developed cooperatively by elementary school teachers, high school teachers, and members of the School of Education faculty.

The faculty wrote books, too, many of them influential in shaping educational thought for years to come. In 1910, Samuel Chester Parker's *A Textbook in the History of Modern Elementary Education* was published. In 1915 came Frank Nugent Freeman's *The Teaching of Handwriting* and Josette Spink's *French Plays for Children.* In 1916, Walter Sargent and Elizabeth Miller brought out their book, *How Children Learn to Draw.* In 1917, *Oral and Written English,* by

Harry O. Gillet, M. C. Potter, and H. Jeschke, appeared. Katherine Stilwell's *The School Printshop* was published in 1919, as was *General Methods of Teaching in the Elementary Schools,* another book by Samuel Chester Parker, which contained many photographs and descriptions of classroom activities carried on in the University Elementary School.

"After." After-school play, referred to through the years as "after," was another innovation that has remained unique. While the elementary school may not have been the first to organize such "after" classes, beginning in 1915, there were few in the nation. A supervisor of play was added to the faculty, and each afternoon from three to four-thirty his duty was to supervise the boys' recreation. The project was financed by the Parents' Association, which contributed $300 yearly. Membership in the play group was voluntary, and the boys came from the middle and upper grades of not only the University Elementary School but also neighboring public and parochial schools. In addition to play, the first groups had classes in printing, woodworking, clay modeling, sewing, and cooking. The last three were later discontinued, and a science class was organized. These classes were carried on from November to March, but the play classes ran all year. In 1918, social dancing—occasionally called "social torture" by the boys—was added for grades six and seven.

"After" has had its ups and downs over the past half century, but it has continued to function, sometimes as part of the school curriculum, sometimes as an adjunct.

The Parents' Association. The Parents' Association continued to be active, keeping its members and other parents informed about the school's activities and progress, innovations and investigations. It also helped to finance extra-curricular activities such as after-school play. Another financial obligation was the art fund, established to provide pictures for corridors and classrooms. The list of projects to which the Association contributed was amazingly long and varied. For example, the report for the year 1909 stated that the Parents' Association, through its Social Fund, contributed $950 to the elementary school for dancing, $70 for special parties, $50 for grade parties, and $80 for the spring festival. In 1910, $750 was contributed to the high school *Daily*, $600 to pay for a teacher of dancing, $100 for music for dances, $50 to the Dramatic Club, $150 to the Debating Club, $200 for parties, and $900 for athletics. The Boys' Club, organized in 1907, and the Girls' Club, organized in 1911, furnished centers for daily social gatherings, and these too were supported by the Parents' Association.

The Association's Home and Education Committee and Social Committee were diligent and enterprising. The first planned the yearly program for the general meetings and the mothers' meetings, and the second supported extra-curricular activities. In 1917 and 1918, during World War I, the Home and Education Committee organized Red Cross and other service work. At the Christmas program in December, 1917, representative students described what they and their classmates had done at home and at school for the men in the armed services, for refugees, for settlements, and for other organizations which were in need of materials and contributions. There were also exhibits of samples of articles made.

This committee, in planning meetings each month, made it possible for the parents to be informed about the academic activities of the schools. The following

This tool shed being built by upper-grade children is still in use in Scammons Garden.

programs for 1916–17 are typical: In October, a report was given on the school surveys conducted by the Department of Education. In November, the Colonel Parker memorial program was held. In December, there were reports on the schools' activities; in January, a display of handwork done by students; and in February, a display of shopwork. In March, the topic was "Science as a Center of the Reorganized High School Course."

THE UNIVERSITY HIGH SCHOOL

Franklin W. Johnson, principal of the high school until the last year of this decade, contributed significantly to the experimentation and research which were going forward there, largely in the fields of mathematics, English, science, manual arts, and the educative social life.

Mathematics. Members of the mathematics faculty continued the research begun earlier under George W. Myers. In 1909, the faculty was carrying on parallel courses in algebra and geometry so as to discover the best possible type of subject matter for secondary students in mathematics. Not all the experimentation, however, was done for the purpose of determining courses of study. In 1913, for instance, Mr. Ernest R. Breslich gave the faculty an account of the experiments carried on in the mathematics department with special reference to students' homework. In the previous year, there had been some criticism of the assigned homework in freshman mathematics, to the effect that students did not understand the assignments clearly enough to be able to do their homework. Mr. Breslich thereupon instituted an experiment in which he used part of the class time for study and for initiating the homework.

Testing, Testing, Testing

Finding that many students did not know how to study, he next set out to discover how they could be helped in their independent study. He instituted a study hour, during which the classroom was open to any student who was having difficulty and wished help. As always, of course, there were those who needed help but never came. Therefore, in the second semester two groups were set up. One group had homework; the other group had no homework, and used the time usually reserved for a discussion of homework for study. Out of this arrangement grew another problem: how to conduct a class organized in this manner and what amounts of homework should be assigned when individual capacities for doing mathematics were so varied.

Thus the ongoing experimentation was taking members of the mathematics department not only into the problems of teaching their subject but also into those of homework and of adjusting teaching and testing to the students' range of abilities. One of Mr. Breslich's co-workers, Raleigh Schorling, made a study of how other schools were providing for individual differences in the teaching of secondary school mathematics. Finding that almost the only provision for the "fast worker" was using him as an instructor or monitor for slow students or assigning him supplementary reading, Mr. Schorling urged that students be registered on the basis of ability. He also suggested such interest-arousing devices as mathematics exhibits, mathematics clubs, and interscholastic mathematics contests. These met with considerable success: A mathematics contest between Hyde Park High School and the University High School generated as much excitement and enthusiasm as a competitive sports event. In fact, a valuable cup was donated to the winning team.

The History of the Laboratory Schools

In 1916, Mr. Breslich and his staff outlined a "Course of Study in Secondary Mathematics in the University High School," an outgrowth of the reorganization which had been continuing since 1903. The course was based on correlation—bringing together closely related subjects, supplementing algebra with geometry and vice versa. Major attention had been given to the first-year course, which the staff felt was now well organized.

Between 1909 and 1916, two textbooks in mathematics were written by members of the department: *Second Year Mathematics for Secondary Schools* by George W. Myers (1910) and Mr. Breslich's *First Year Mathematics for Secondary Schools* (1915).

The Sciences. Combination and correlation of subject-matter areas were being tried in science courses also. The teachers of general science experimented with a single course that combined botany, zoology, physiography, and physics for first- and second-year students in the high school. A report on the experiment, made in April, 1912, received considerable attention. The material was chosen for its significance to the students in terms of the life they then knew, rather than preparing them for adult years. The material was well correlated, and the boundary lines between the sciences were made as inconspicuous as possible.

Academic Standards. Mr. Johnson, the principal, made a comparative study of the grades of first-year high school students from different elementary schools. He found that in the autumn quarter, 1910, the freshmen from the University Elementary School were greatly superior to those from other schools in Latin, mathematics, French, German, and design. In English they were somewhat inferior, and decidedly inferior in history and science. It is easy to imagine the agitation that

84

the results of the study must have caused among the seventh- and eighth-grade teachers of English, history, and science.

This same method of appraisal was carried to higher levels. Just as the quality of teaching done in the latter years of the elementary school was tested by the students' grades during the first year of high school, so their grades in the first year of college served as a test of the quality of the high school teaching. Mr. Johnson, in his report to the president, confessed that the results of the tests showed the teaching to be less than satisfactory. Steps to remedy the situation would be instituted immediately, he explained, not only to improve standards of scholarship but to effect a closer correlation between the elementary school and the high school.

Using students' grades to test the efficacy of previous teaching revealed another problem—variations in different teachers' systems of grading. When Mr. Johnson made a study of these variations, he certainly opened a Pandora's box of troubles. It was difficult to compare the grades given by different teachers, since some were prone to give higher grades than others, and just as difficult to compare the grades given by different teachers to the same children. Mr. Johnson's study led to much discussion and was widely quoted and used.

The principal's promise to raise the standards of the high school led the faculty to propose that students whose grades persistently fell below the standard, which was 60 percent, should be excluded. However, if a student made a grade of 55 percent, he would be given a conditional promotion and allowed to go on with the work of the following quarter for four weeks, at which time he would take an examination. If he passed, the conditional promotion was offset. The plan was put into effect, but soon a question arose in the minds of some of the faculty: Did it spur students to do better work? Hence a study of the results of the plan was made by Walter Morgan in 1911. He found that if a student managed to get a higher grade in one subject, this increase was offset by a falling off in some other subject. In fact, Mr. Morgan found that the conditional promotion had a "negative moral influence."

Other plans were suggested. As each was tried and found ineffective, another would be adopted and, after trial, be scrutinized and reviewed. In his "Editorial Comment" in January, 1916, Mr. Judd listed three "legitimate devices for securing the right kind of economy": "excess credit" for high-grade work, rapid promotion for the best students, and careful selection of essentials in all courses.

In 1913, the enrollment in the high school was limited to four hundred. This meant that superior students could be selected from a larger group of applicants and that high standards could thus be set and maintained. The next year's report noted that there was now a waiting list of applicants and that superior preparation was made the basis for admission. In 1907, the tuition had been increased from $120 to $150; in 1914, it was increased again to $200.

Social Life. While many means were being explored to keep academic standards high, the emphasis was by no means on all work and no play. The University High School's outstanding social program for a "truly educative life" was well in advance of social programs in high schools generally. One of the basic tenets of the school from its earliest days was the all-round development of its students, with provision for social as well as academic growth.

86

Testing, Testing, Testing

Societies and clubs there were in number. In 1915–16, the following were listed: University High School Literary Society, Discussion Club, Engineering Club, Sophomore Literary Society, Public Speaking Club, Science Club, French Club, Sketch Club, Girls' Glee Club, Junior Girls' Society, and the newly organized Senior Girls' Society as well as the staff of the *University High School Daily* and the staff of the *Midway*. The *Daily* had four editors; the *Midway*, which came out every six weeks, was composed of about thirty-five pages of stories, plays, and verse, all contributed by the students.

Besides the societies and clubs there were the dances. Two parties—"two gorgeous parties"—were given special mention in the *Correlator* for 1915, 1916, and 1917. One was the annual Christmas party, for which the parents provided the decorations, refreshments, and music for dancing and to which the students brought gifts for the children of the settlement or United Charities. The other party was held sometime in the second semester. One year it was the Washington's Birthday dance; another year it was the last Friday afternoon dance on March 5. In 1917, it was a spring party, held in "beautiful new Ida Noyes Hall."

Athletics. In 1916, Mr. Judd wrote in an editorial "the social and athletic activities of our students are quite as fundamental as the strictly academic activities." Through inter-class as well as inter-school contests, an effort was made to involve the active participation of as many students as possible. The girls' basketball team played against girls' teams from other schools, and the boys' football, baseball, and track teams competed in the same way. For both boys and girls there were inter-class games and contests in golf, tennis, hockey, baseball, basketball, track, gymnastics, and swimming. Let-

87

ters and awards were presented each year to those who participated regularly.

THE SCHOOLS AND THE WAR

It was amazing, considering the many demands made on them, that students found time for the host of contributions they made to the war effort in 1916–18. While the activities of the high school students were more varied, the children in the elementary school played their part in purchasing thrift stamps, subscribing to Liberty Loan drives, collecting book and phonograph records for army and navy camps, and contributing to the Committee on Armenian and Syrian Relief.

In the spring of 1916, twenty-four University High School boys went to Pendleton, Indiana, to work on the farms in that vicinity. In the beginning, these particular city youngsters did not know the difference "between a hay loader and a pitchfork," but they learned quickly and performed astonishingly well. The manual training instructor, E. T. Filbey, who had charge of the boys, spent his entire time going from farm to farm on a motorcycle provided by one of them, giving instruction and encouragement wherever needed. Each boy contributed his wages, after traveling expenses had been deducted, to a fund for war relief. A total of $2,200 was raised to purchase an ambulance and provide a driver for one year for the American Ambulance Service in France. Rowland Campbell, of the class of 1916, was sent as driver.

In 1917, the students supported ten war orphans through an organization called the Fatherless Children of France. Two victrolas, more than two hundred records, and 1,087 books were collected for army and navy camps. Six thousand surgical dressings were prepared, and 150 articles were knitted for the Red Cross. Students contributed or secured $70,000 in subscriptions to the Third Liberty Loan, and bought $6,000 worth of thrift stamps. Sixty boys were enrolled in the United States Working Reserve.

In 1918, not only was the University High School company for military drill formed, but the facilities of the high school shops were used by the University when it undertook to train a hundred drafted men to be army mechanics. At the end of a six-week course, the men went into service and a hundred more took their places.

Sympathy for France ran high, and registration in French classes was heavy, while in German classes it fell off perceptibly. In May, 1917, Marshal Joffre and Monsieur Viviani visited the University, and pupils of the two schools were excused from classes to see the dignitaries, heads of the French mission. The children lined the Midway and sang the "Marseillaise" as the visitors rode by in an open automobile.

These contributions to World War I were in line with a school tradition for generosity, both to the community and to national projects. In the immediate community, the Mary McDowell Settlement, the Hyde Park Neighborhood Club, the Community Fund, the Home for Destitute Crippled Children, other children's hospitals, day nurseries, public kindergartens, and primary schools in deprived areas of Chicago—all were recipients of school gifts. In later years, national and international organizations, such as the World Student Service Fund, the American Red Cross, American Friends Service Committee, the United Nations Appeal, and the United Nations International Children's Fund

(UNICEF) received contributions. Individual grades gave money to CARE and the Chicago Heart Association, books to a school in the mountains of Kentucky and to the International Library for Children in Germany, and toys to a needy kindergarten group in the city. Through the years Laboratory School students have learned the grace of sharing, the satisfaction of giving, and consideration for one's neighbors, near and far. Even though the schools are private, their students have been world-interested and world-oriented—in Mr. Jackman's words, contributing to "quality of life, as this expresses itself in . . . helpfulness, gentleness of spirit, sensitiveness to the rights of others."

READING FOR PLEASURE: THE SCHOOL LIBRARY

To us of the present day, who have a great number of books, paperbacks and hardbacks, available for our pleasure as well as our information, it is difficult to think that such reading in schools could ever have been unusual. Yet it was unusual back in 1910—sufficiently so to merit emphasis and attention in a publication. Mr. Judd, in one of his editorials for the *Elementary School Teacher,* wrote of supplementary reading in the University High School:

> We are all convinced that supplementary reading has come to stay. The best kind of supplementary reading is that which children get by going to books in the library. . . . Teachers [he added] should learn to use books and guide children in the use of books.

The Schools had a library, a joint one, established in

1903 when Blaine Hall was built. It is to be inferred from class assignments that the Dewey and Parker schools also had classroom libraries, but the first central library came with Blaine. Room 200, now the elementary school library, served as library for the School of Education, the University High School, and the University Elementary School. Teachers borrowed books and took them to the classrooms for supplementary as well as textbook reading. Pupils also went to the central library, but not so frequently or freely as they do today.

By 1909, the joint library was too small to accommodate the books on hand, and a reading-study room was needed for the high school. So Room 117 in Blaine was equipped as such a library, with a teacher in charge. This was the University High School's first library of its own. According to some sources, it was the first of its kind in the nation.

An experiment in leading students to enjoy reading was tried in 1918–19, when the sophomore English laboratory was set up. This innovation was important enough to be included in the School of Education news items in the December, 1919, *School Review.*

> Students were seated somewhat informally about a room in which were book shelves containing about 500 books. . . . The room was organized and conducted so that an atmosphere of restfulness and leisure prevailed. During two regular class periods each week the students came to the room for the purpose of reading what they liked.

The University High School was well in the fore-front then, as it is at the present, in the use of library materials and in the extension of supplementary reading. It was a school library to which other schools, as well as teachers and librarians, looked for ideas.

A problem which had engaged schoolmen and industrialists for more than twenty-five years was that of the trade school—the place of manual training and, later, vocational training, in the schools of the country. The University High School, because the Chicago Manual Training School was one of its components, was more or less involved in the controversy.

Ever since the first manual training schools had been established in the United States, manufacturers had put more and more pressure on these schools to provide their plants with trained workers. Opposed to the manufacturers were two groups—the industrial workers themselves, who were afraid the manufacturers would hire inexperienced labor, and educators, who wanted to retain the manual training schools' program of general and liberal culture.

Mr. Belfield was of course one of the latter. A Latin scholar, he insisted on training in the classics and on courses in chemistry, physics, English, and foreign languages in addition to manual training. In the Chicago Manual Training School, the schedule included a half day of solid academic work plus shopwork, drawing, and physical education—quite a different schedule from that of other early manual training schools. Mr. Filbey, manual training instructor in the University High School during the years of Mr. Judd, stated in an interview in 1959 that when the Chicago Manual Training School became part of the University High School, manual training "was done clearly in the interests of supplementing and enriching education of young people who would later do college work."

Three men connected with the School of Education and the University High School—Charles Judd, Walter Sargent, and Frank M. Leavitt—were very influential in the field of industrial arts through their writings and teachings. Mr. Judd did not favor two high schools, one for technical training and one for general education, as many educators advocated. He wanted vocational high schools which would be a part of the public school system and which would prepare students for citizenship as well as for industry. With Mr. Belfield, he urged a general and liberal education for manual training students.

Mr. Sargent was greatly interested in the manual arts in the secondary schools, for reasons unique at that time. To quote Mr. Filbey again:

> Mr. Sargent was one of the country's outstanding exponents of art education beginning in the early grades. He insisted that art did not depend on any special talent—that anyone could learn to sketch and draw for enjoyment and appreciation. Art, as Mr. Sargent saw it, covered almost all of the individual's environment: art effects in the home, utensils in the kitchen. . . . His leadership not only in art but in manual training tied the two together.

Mr. Leavitt, who came to the School of Education in 1910 as associate professor of industrial education, was a nationally known industrial educator. He had received his training in the School of Mechanic Arts at the Massachusetts Institute of Technology and was greatly interested in vocational and pre-vocational education, especially in what vocational and industrial education could do for (in his words) the "83% of the pupils who conclude their school life before the 17th year." He was concerned with the potential dropouts who could not keep abreast of the academic work but could, through industrial education, achieve some success and thus be salvaged for a productive life. He too urged that instruction in the manual arts be made part of the high school program and as fully and freely recognized as any other subject in the curriculum. He did not want vocational training to be considered appropriate only for students who could not do academic work. Rather it should be "administered in the spirit of impartial sympathy," with continual encouragement for students showing interest, accomplishment, or improvement.

A number of experiments were carried on in the University High School shops. While these did not directly affect the University High School student population, the facilities of the school were used, faculty members were involved, and the results were watched with interest. One industrial experimental class was composed of potential dropouts from the public schools. They attended school during the whole summer for seven and a half hours daily, taking both shop and academic work. The parents of some of these students doubted that the work had much value because the boys liked it so well!

Another experiment, initiated by Mr. Leavitt, was also designed to salvage public school boys who did not get along satisfactorily in the academic program. The facilities of the high school were used in training twenty such boys—wood shop, forge shop, foundry, machine shop, and drafting rooms. The boys took academic subjects too—mathematics, history, science, and English. Mr. Judd, in his 1913–14 report to the president, made this comment on the experiment:

> The importance of this experiment lies in the fact that material is being accumulated which will illustrate the methods that should be adopted in supplementing ordinary school work so as to furnish the proper training for boys who heretofore have been entirely out of sympathy and contact with ordinary school training.

Without doubt, the experimentation carried on by Mr. Judd, Mr. Sargent, and Mr. Leavitt, plus their writings, influenced the place and aim of manual training in the high schools.

AN ERA ENDS

Franklin Johnson was given a leave of absence for the wartime year 1918–19, and, commissioned as major, engaged in educational services for the Surgeon General's Office. Morton Snyder was appointed principal of the High School in his place, and four professors from the School of Education shared the administrative supervision of the school.

Since Mr. Johnson did not return to the high school after the war, some reorganization was necessary, and on July 1, 1919, Mr. Judd appointed Henry Clinton Morrison as superintendent in charge of both schools. Another era in their history was coming to a close. The experimentation of course went on, as well as some testing, but with the new superintendent a new direction was established.

The History of the Laboratory Schools

In retrospect, the decade 1909–19 was marked by a fever of testing and experimentation in both schools, particularly the elementary school; by the raising of academic standards in the high school; by the impact of World War I; by an increased use of libraries, especially in the high school; by continued efforts to provide an "educative social life"; and by the influence of the School of Education on the place of manual training in the nation's high schools. The schools continued to be laboratories, preeminent in the education field, and what went on there, what was written, discussed, and lectured about, had an impact even in the hinterlands.

Six

Between the Great War
and the Great Depression
1919–1931

In the history of the Laboratory Schools, the periods
1909–19 and 1919–31, though divided somewhat arbi-
trarily, are each characterized by some dominating
movement or emphasis which of course did not come
to an end at the close of the period but merely tapered
off. Just as 1909–19 had been, among other things,
a decade of extensive scientific testing and research
(which did not terminate in 1919), so 1919–31 was an
era during which a concise, detailed method of teaching was developed and the terms "unit" and "mastery"
became popular.

The man whose name was almost synonymous with
those terms was Henry Clinton Morrison, who brought
them into the educational limelight and whose method
of teaching spread through the schools of the nation.
Mr. Morrison came to the University of Chicago in
1919 as professor of school administration and superintendent of the Laboratory Schools. Mr. Judd con-

tinued as head of the Department of Education, but felt he could not devote enough time to the schools and needed someone to take over their supervision.

Mr. Morrison had had an extensive background in teaching and administration. He had been a high school principal, a city superintendent of schools, state superintendent of New Hampshire schools, and assistant secretary to the Connecticut Board of Education. In his thirteen years as superintendent of New Hampshire schools he had carried on various educational experiments, and hence welcomed the opportunity to use the Laboratory Schools for further experimental work. He had definite ideas about education, especially how to teach and get results, and at the Laboratory Schools he tested these ideas, refining and enlarging on them. His book, *The Practice of Teaching in the Secondary Schools,* appeared first in mimeographed form in 1924, and in hard covers two years later. It caused a tremendous sensation in the educational world.

Like his predecessors, Mr. Morrison protested against dull memorizing of facts, lesson-learning, and pages-to-be-covered. He argued for principles to be understood, appreciations to be attained, changes in attitude to be brought about, and gains in special abilities or skills to be achieved. Having set up specific objectives, he believed that the material used in achieving these objectives should be organized into manageable portions called *units.* He had several definitions for a unit, among them this one given in his discussion of the teaching of science:

A unit is a comprehensive and significant aspect of the environment or of an organized science, capable of being understood rather than capable merely of being remembered. (*The Practice of Teaching in the Secondary Schools,* page 182.)

The unit idea spread amazingly fast. After the publication of Mr. Morrison's book, school superintendents, principals, teachers, students, publishers, authors of textbooks, and writers of educational articles enrolled in his classes. The idea of units was not totally new, nor was it originated by Mr. Morrison, but certainly he popularized it—to the extent that, over the following years, there were few textbooks whose contents were not organized in units.

Mr. Morrison's method of teaching, his technique, began with the unit because it was through the unit that pupils worked, but the key word was *mastery,* the ultimate objective of each unit. The pupils were to attain *full* mastery—not half-mastery, not 60 or 70 percent (what he called "putative mastery").

Mastery was reached by means of a definite, precise technique. First of all, the teacher had to determine in advance the understanding, or appreciation, or power that must be attained, and plan the unit, selecting the material which would lead the pupil to the desired appreciation or understanding. Next, he had to decide on the minimum essentials every pupil must master. Following that, in grades above the third, extra work had to be planned for pupils who finished the minimum assignments and passed the tests.

After this preparation, the teacher drew up a guide sheet on which were listed all the pupils' reading references. From that point on, five precise steps were followed:

1. *Exploration*—finding out, by tests or questioning, what the pupils already knew about the projected unit.

A sand table replica of an eighth- or ninth-century tournament. This may have been built as a result of historical studies or through enjoyment of literature from the period.

2. *Presentation*—an overview of the unit given orally to the pupils, followed by a test to determine whether or not they understood what the unit would encompass. If they did not, it was the teacher's duty to present the overview again, and give another test.

3. *Assimilation*—all the activities in which the pupils took part in reaching the objective, such activities as experiments, written exercises, drawing, construction, mathematical exercises, and, most important of all, reading. Tests were given from time to time during the assimilation period. If a pupil failed a test, he was retaught and re-tested. If he failed again, the process was repeated until he reached the goal—that is, attained mastery. "Half learning is soon forgotten. Mastery abides," wrote Mr. Morrison.

4. *Organization*—the summing up of the unit by the pupils, with the help of the teacher.

5. *Recitation*—in which the pupils presented the unit in parts or as a whole. In the intermediate grades, this was often done at an assembly where pupils gave talks or dramatizations or showed correlated artwork.

This, then, was the technique which brought hundreds of students, teachers, principals, and administrators to the Department of Education and countless visitors to the Laboratory Schools. Requests for guide sheets began to pour in as more and more teachers in outlying areas were requested to plan units for their work.

Mr. Morrison had a strong influence on textbooks for the intermediate grades and high schools. After 1926, the word *chapter* began to disappear, to be replaced by the word *unit*. In science and social studies especially, the subject matter was nearly always in units.

Constructing a unit was indeed an exercise and an

education for the teacher—as well as the pupil. The teacher had to determine the outcome, the purpose of the unit, know the material which went into it, and read all the assigned references and the supplementary books. Day-by-day, page-by-page assignments were a thing of the past, since, with the aid of the guide sheets, the pupil was encouraged to work at his own speed. The period of assimilation alone might go on for a week or longer.

Another important task for the teacher who used the unit technique was test construction. Since all the steps in the unit had to be tested and re-tested in order to determine when and where re-teaching was necessary, the teacher came to have extensive experience with true-false, completion, multiple-choice, and essay tests—their construction, trial, revision, and re-revision. The tests were diagnostic, and no grades were given on them. However, the results were charted question by question, item by item. The only exceptions to this testing procedure were in science, where a completed experiment showed the pupils' understanding; in physical education, where a certain performance showed the pupil's ability; or in literature or art, where an original piece of work—essay or poem, drawing or painting— showed that the pupil had attained an appreciation.

In Mr. Morrison's technique there was no place for homework or for "lesson-learning." In one of his directives in 1920–21 he warned that:

> . . . some teachers are relapsing into the old custom of assigning regular home-work and into its deplorable counterpart, routine lesson-learning. I request this custom come to a close.

As has been stated, no grades were given on the tests,

because they were purely diagnostic. If a pupil had not learned what was taught him, or what he was exposed to, he was not to be dismissed with a low grade. Mr. Morrison was likewise adamant against grading test papers in terms of percentages. He wrote:

> Papers should not be graded. We are working in terms of securing in the pupils understanding, clear thinking, and some kind of specific power, and are not interested in any given amount of work to be covered.

He was also adamant about pupils making full use of their time. In 1921–22, he had printed forms of the Sustained Application Profile Sheet made available to the teachers. The sheet, devised by Hannah Logasa, the high school librarian, and used in her conferences with students on their study habits, appealed strongly to Mr. Morrison. It was an ingenious device for charting a pupil's application to his work—unknown to the pupil. The teacher, watch in hand, simply kept track of how long a pupil concentrated on his work.

Later a similar profile was made for a whole class. Some person other than the teacher counted the number of pupils paying attention during each interval. Mr. Morrison firmly believed that each class must give 100 percent active attention to the work and that the teacher must be able to keep all the youngsters fully occupied without wasteful interruptions.

Mr. Morrison believed that if the Laboratory Schools were to live up to their name, data must be recorded every day on all teaching. At first, monthly reports were required, but, by 1925, the requirement was reduced to two—one at the end of each semester. Teachers, however, had to keep daily records, since the reports included summaries of units, guide sheets, extra reading lists, tests and test results, records of re-teaching, reports of extra work or reading, graphs and statistical charts, and personal reports of pupils who were outstanding or were having noticeable difficulties. The data gathered from 1919 to 1933, when such reports were terminated, represent untold hours of work by the teachers. The amount is not only voluminous; it is staggering. For the elementary school, there are as many as fifteen volumes for one year, some volumes with well over a thousand pages.

Auxiliary to the unit-and-mastery technique was the addition of a remedial teacher and a school psychologist to the faculty and the establishment of the Records Office.

The Remedial Teacher. The technique stressed individual attention to pupils and individual teaching, for each pupil set his own pace in accomplishing the goals of the unit. Mr. Morrison believed that all children except defectives could achieve mastery. Since there were always a few who had considerable difficulty, the grade teacher referred these cases to the remedial teacher, who continued as part of the faculty for many years. In the beginning, the remedial teacher worked with children who had early reading difficulties, later with those who had trouble in other subject areas.

The Records Office. As a result of Mr. Morrison's emphasis on the importance of the individual pupil, a sizable amount of information was accumulated on each child—folders that included his written papers, artwork, health history, information on his interests and special abilities, and what Mr. Morrison called his "school, history, including temperament, indolence, school behavior, mentality, intelligence, and leadership."

In the school year 1920–21, this material was kept in case files set up in the homerooms. At the end of the year, the information in the file folders was transferred to the Records Office. This was the beginning of a system of extensive record-keeping which has continued to the present time and has been adopted by many other schools.

A SIX-YEAR ELEMENTARY SCHOOL

Mr. Morrison's report to the president for the year 1919–20 announced that two important changes in the organization of the Laboratory Schools would be made during the following year. The first was "the transfer of the seventh grade from the Elementary School to the jurisdiction of the High School"; the second was the addition of a number of junior college courses to the high school curriculum. Judging from the few reports available, the shift of the seventh grade to the high school was made without much discussion, except to ask the seventh-grade teachers if they were willing to be transferred to the high school jurisdiction. Thus the elementary school became a six-year school (not including the kindergarten) in the autumn of 1920, making the high school a five-year school. The seventh-grade pupils were first called sub-freshmen and later pre-freshmen.

ABILITY GROUPING

The 1920's brought many more changes. Whenever a new idea was tried and did not bring about desired results, it was abandoned and replaced by another. Some ideas were theoretically good but proved ineffectual when put into practice. Before 1920, for example, there had been half-year grade designations, such as 3A and 3B, but in that year a full-year grade designation was adopted. Another change came in 1921–22, when departmental teaching was instituted in the intermediate grades. The plan was based on Mr. Dewey's idea that teachers specializing in one field could give the pupils the richest background. Each homeroom teacher taught one subject to all the pupils in grades four, five, and six. One homeroom teacher taught all the mathematics classes, another all the history, another the geography, and so on. In addition, there were special teachers of science, art, French, and printing.

Departmental teaching had its advantages, but it afforded little opportunity for the correlation of subjects, so within a few years the plan was again changed. By 1925, there were two groups, A and B, in each grade, and two teachers. One taught history and geography to both groups, the other mathematics and language arts. The idea of ability grouping was good theoretically, as it was economical to teach the fast workers and the slower workers separately. In practice, however, it was less than successful. The B's received limited stimulation from each other; there was a discouraged, defeatist attitude among them, an I'm-in-the-dumb-group feeling. Their parents were also unhappy—for one reason, because the B's did not get French. So in 1931, the A and B groups were eliminated and two parallel groups were set up in each grade, both of which studied French. The ability-grouping practice that had become common over the nation began to be questioned, since the Laboratory Schools had tried it and found it unsatisfactory.

Between War and Depression

The testing program continued into the 1920's, but not with the same intensity. Tests formulated earlier were put into use. A program of testing silent and oral reading in the first seven grades was begun in 1920–21. Silent-reading ability was tested by the Courtis Silent Reading and the Monroe Standard Reading tests, and oral-reading ability by the Gray Standardized Reading Paragraphs. Diagnostic charts were made for every grade, indicating each pupil's accomplishments. Dean William S. Gray gave half of his time during the University's autumn and winter quarters in 1921–22 to a study of individual reading difficulties in the elementary school. One of the grade teachers, who devoted her days to testing, diagnosing difficulties, and providing special help, became the first remedial teacher in the elementary school.

In the spring quarter of 1920, the kindergarten children were tested for mental ability, using the Stanford Revision of the Binet-Simon Scale. By that time kindergarten was beginning to be recognized as an integral part of the elementary school, as witness a news item in the *Elementary School Teacher* for September, 1919:

> Samuel Chester Parker's book on *General Methods of Teaching in the Elementary Schools* is among the first in which the material is organized on the assumption that the Kindergarten and first six grades constitute a closely coordinated unit in public school organization.

A LIBRARY FOR THE INTERMEDIATE GRADES

One of Mr. Morrison's terms, "reading adaptation," was used extensively in the primary grades. This adaptation was revealed, he explained, "when a child will of his own volition, select books and straight way take on a characteristic and readily identifiable attitude of absorption." Primary-grade teachers were on the alert for signs of reading adaptation in each child. To encourage it, they made sure a wide selection of interesting books was available to all the children. Every classroom had its reading or library table, and the teachers kept records of what the children read.

By the time pupils had finished the third grade, Mr. Morrison believed, they would have achieved the adaptation and would then be ready to read silently by themselves. Therefore, they must have access to many books for free reading, and this meant access to a library. As mentioned earlier, in the autumn of 1921, a library and reading room for grades four, five, and six was set up in Room 108 of Blaine Hall and stocked with about a thousand books from the juvenile collection in the School of Education library. Fairy tales and other fiction, literature, biography, history, and books on science made up the interesting array. Periodicals—the *Youth's Companion, Literary Digest, American Boy, Popular Mechanics, St. Nicholas,* and *Junior Red Cross Magazine*—were added, as were reference sets.

A Laboratory School grade teacher, Evangeline Colburn, was asked to set up the reading room and plan the investigations to be carried on. Since elementary school libraries or reading rooms were very uncommon, she had an open field, and the pattern she established was followed for many years.

Born of the importance which Mr. Morrison attached to wide reading, the library's organization was distinctive and individual. It was not a copy of any other library reading room. Great freedom was permitted. A pupil could choose any book he wanted and read as much of it as he wished. No book reports were required, and the only record asked for was a list of the books read at home and at school and the date when each book (or part of it) was finished. A self-charging system, which freed the teacher from a time-consuming routine, was initiated in December, 1921, and is still in use today. All the pupils in the three grades came to the library for their reading classes, five half-hours a week. "The teacher's work," wrote the librarian in the *University Elementary School Reports,* "is with the individuals, aiding, guiding them as needed, and sometimes merely observing them."

Like the high school library, the elementary school library began as a reading room, and the librarian was the reading teacher. The idea of a library that served the whole school as a resource and study center, as well as a reading center, came later. But in the early 1920's the elementary school library provided one of the earliest and finest demonstrations of the rich role that a library can play in the reading program. It attracted visitors from near and far—persons who were curious about the freedom of the children, their tastes and interests in books, the books most read, and the variety provided.

The History of the Laboratory Schools

PUBLICATIONS

One may wonder how the Laboratory School teachers ever found time to write textbooks, manuals, articles for pedagogical publications, monographs, and book reviews, but write they did, and their output included textbooks in French, science, mathematics, social science, and English. A diligent graduate student, working on his doctoral dissertation, once listed all the publications written during the twenty-five years from 1903 to 1928 by teachers in the Laboratory Schools, by University students who had used pupils for tests and research, and by the School of Education faculty who had carried on experiments in the Laboratory Schools. The list contains more than two hundred articles in pedagogical magazines written by teachers in the Laboratory Schools, about ninety articles by members of the School of Education faculty on studies made in the Schools, and about forty textbooks written by Laboratory School teachers, not to mention monographs, manuals, contributions to yearbooks, editorials, reports of conferences, book reviews, and tests. More than twenty graduate students did research on Laboratory School pupils to secure material for their master's theses.

No one has undertaken to compile a similar list for the years since 1928, but if it is ever made without doubt it will reveal equally rich contributions to education and an equally far-reaching influence of the University's Laboratory Schools.

Between War and Depression

The Schools had long needed a gymnasium. A temporary one had been built when Colonel Parker brought his faculty to the University of Chicago, and the building had been known as "Gym Temp" ever since. In June, 1927, ground was broken for the Bernard Edward Sunny Gymnasium. Its donor, Mr. Sunny, a director and chairman of the board of the Illinois Bell Telephone Company from 1922 to 1930, had been interested in the Laboratory Schools for many years, and his five grandchildren had been pupils there from kindergarten on. The gymnasium was completed during the 1928–29 school year. Among its excellent facilities, the swimming pool stood out above all else. In the 1930 *Correlator,* a student wrote enthusiastically about the new gymnasium:

> Going indoors, maybe we can see the pool which is one of the most beautiful natatoriums in the city.
>
> You know, when I look at Gym Temp and then compare it to this masterpiece, I wonder how we ever managed to do the few things that the fire department let us do. . . . There is even a large sliding door with which we can make two gyms out of one.

The physical education staff was doubled, and all students were included in the daily physical education program. Morning and afternoon recesses in the elementary school were abolished, but no one missed them because they were replaced by an hour of gymnasium or plays and games.

Lloyd B. Sharp, the new head of the physical education program, inaugurated the first "Sunny Play Day," in June, 1930. The entire school—pupils, parents, and teachers—took part in baseball games, races, and other contests, followed by a picnic supper in Scammon Garden. Play Day was an institution for many years, giving parents of children in different grades an excellent opportunity to become acquainted. As the school enrollment increased, there was no longer enough space for a large all-school picnic, but each class has had an annual picnic supper and games, or a get-together of some kind, down to the present time. (When a family has two or three or four children in the Schools, fathers have been known to joke about eating picnic fare for three and four evenings a week during Play Day time.)

The physical education program included the health program. On the two days preceding the opening of school each autumn, the Schools' two physicians and members of the physical education staff examined every pupil—his weight, height, throat, heart, lungs, vision, and hearing. Into the report went parents' accounts of their children's illnesses, accidents, operations, vaccinations, or treatments during the past year. Another, more complete examination was made on or near each pupil's birthday.

Since this was before inoculations for communicable diseases were prevalent, classes were "quarantined" whenever a pupil came down with a communicable disease and thus exposed others in the class. "Quarantine" meant that the exposed children would be separated from the others in the lunchroom, in plays and games, and elsewhere. The practice was later abolished, but it was an indication of the Schools' care and concern for their pupils' physical health.

The physical education and health programs were

outstanding at the time, both for their attention to the individual child and for the detailed compilations of the health histories which they produced. Changes have come with the passing years, because of inoculations, antibiotics, and other forms of preventive medicine, but care for the pupil's well-being continues undiminished.

REPORTING TO PARENTS

No part of the Laboratory Schools' program has gone through so many variations as that having to do with reports to parents, and in almost no area have so many devices been tried, only to be succeeded by others. Whether or not the perfect reporting method will ever be found is not known, but the different methods used in the Schools are of interest not only in themselves but also because they were adopted by many other schools.

In a letter to his faculty in 1921, Mr. Gillet, principal of the elementary school, gave directions for making reports. Cards for each pupil were kept in the office of the principal. The teachers were asked to indicate on these cards whether the pupil's work was complete or incomplete. Also, for the information of the principal, the grades A, B, C, D, and E were to be entered, to indicate the pupil's interest, effort, and application. Some explanatory remarks were requested, but these too were for Mr. Gillet's information only. Finally, the teachers were asked to mark the pupil's work in each subject as satisfactory or unsatisfactory. Then Mr. Gillet himself made all the reports to parents—in conference if a parent so requested.

In describing their pupils' work, the teachers were

not required to follow any particular pattern. Each teacher wrote about the personal qualities of the child that seemed important to him. One teacher might emphasize industry; another, responsibility; another, originality or persistence; and so on. Thus the reports could not be used to study a pupil's growth in behavior, since one teacher might mention a quality which the next teacher ignored. In 1925, a psychologist was added to the faculty, and the position became a permanent one. Four years later, the psychologist undertook to devise a personality-rating form for the elementary school. From the reports, she listed the qualities or attributes most frequently mentioned by the teachers, then made a check list to be used in reporting on each pupil's growth. It was intended to save time for the teachers, but the list, when completed, was long and detailed. Teachers found it frustrating, since judging attributes on a scale is a difficult thing to do. Also, the resulting report did not give parents a clear picture of the pupil's application or of his work in general. The check list was used for only a few years but it was the first of many attempts to make reporting more effective and of real value to the parents, other teachers, and the pupils.

In the high school, the five-point letter system, A, B, C, D, E, was used. In 1919–20, a system of excess credits was devised for students who were efficient in classwork and could handle added responsibility. For example, credits in social science were given for special studies on suggested topics, for writing historical papers, and for reading biographies. The students were avid for such recognition and became far too zealous as excess-credit collectors. In the following year, this plan was discontinued.

The next plan was that of weighted credits. Mastery

High school clubs exhibited their projects in the library, which was located on the second floor of Belfield Hall. Aviation was of current interest in these early days of airplane development.

of the minimum essentials of a unit was designated by the letter M, but there was another designation, N, for students who also did supplementary projects, and still another, R, for those who not only did supplementary projects but original and independent work as well. Moreover, the M appeared in three forms: M_1 indicated easy mastery with no re-teaching; M_2, some re-teaching; and M_3, difficulty in reaching mastery and much re-teaching.

By February, 1926, there had been another turn of the wheel. Reports to parents of high school students were now made in the form of a letter, which was actually a composite of progress reports contributed by each teacher. No grades were given; instead, there was a statement about the student's work. The letter was signed by the principal or assistant principal. This form of reporting continued for some time.

MR. MORRISON RESIGNS

At the end of the school year 1927–28, Mr. Morrison resigned as superintendent of the Laboratory Schools in order to devote his time to University teaching and to writing. He left behind him voluminous reports written by the teachers, and records on every pupil in the Schools—master cards with health data, social histories, test results, and documentary materials. He also left with the teachers who had come under his supervision a heightened consciousness of their obligation to every pupil in their classes. The semi-annual work reports which Mr. Morrison had instituted continued to be required until 1933.

Between War and Depression

During 1919–31, along with unit construction, guide sheet organization, the testing program, and publications, there was also much research and experimentation.

In 1921–22, the Psychology Department of the School of Education began two research studies. The first interpreted the results of psycho-physical tests given to a large number of elementary school pupils on or near each pupil's birthday. The other, designed to follow the development of bones as an index to anatomical development, involved securing and measuring radiographs of the metacarpal bones of each pupil's right hand to learn the degree of ossification. The study was carried on over several years, and the results were made available to students.

In 1926, research and investigations in remedial reading were carried into the high school and continued there for the next ten years. They began with a general survey of reading achievement, especially in sub-freshman, freshman, and sophomore classes. From 1926 to 1929, individual remedial work was done, but from 1929 to 1931 the first experiments in group remedial training were tried, especially among sub-freshmen and freshmen. The study was begun by a graduate student. In 1931, however, the Schools' psychologist took over the investigation of the effectiveness of group remedial reading instruction.

In the school year 1929–30, Mr. Frank N. Freeman of the School of Education conducted an investigation in several cities to find out whether the typewriter could be used as a supplement to handwriting in grades one through six. The University Elementary School's primary grades were included in the study. Experimental and control groups were set up, and typewriters made available to the experimental group—one machine to about four pupils. The teachers gave the pupils simple directions, and the pupils did their typing in hunt-and-peck fashion. They were entranced by the machines and used them as often as possible. Mr. Freeman found that using a typewriter neither slowed down the pupils' development of skill in handwriting, nor did it make their handwriting less legible. In fact the machines actually seemed to stimulate the pupils' production of written work. They not only wrote more but even turned in more handwritten papers than did pupils in the control group.

CLUBS AND INTEREST GROUPS

The University High School had more interest clubs than most high schools four times its size. Each year new ones were added to those of long standing. In 1924, the University Hi-Y was founded and the Writers Club organized. In 1926, the U-Hi Forum became the U-Hi Club. In 1927, the Purple Mask had its beginning—and end—and the Science Club was organized for underclassmen who had previously belonged to the Engineering Club. In 1928, the Movie Club was begun, and in 1929, there were three new ones: Aviation, Rifle, and Know Chicago. (One of the students in the Aviation Club built a two-passenger plane and gave it to the club members.) The Midway Glider Club was also organized at that time. In 1928, there were about twenty-four different activities, including clubs, in a school of fewer than six hundred students.

Between War and Depression

The Parents' Association, now more than twenty years old, had always been a growing, thriving, active, interested organization. The programs of its general meetings in the mid-1920's indicate the interests and activities of the Schools. Consider this sampling of program titles: "Educative and Administrative Undertakings of the University Laboratory Schools," "Adjusting Instruction to the Individual Needs of Pupils," "Tests—What They Are and How We Use Them," "Teaching of English in the Laboratory Schools," "Nutrition and Learning," "Science in the Elementary School," "Reading in the Elementary School," and "Mathematics in the Elementary School." The parents set up the programs and also planned demonstrations of classwork in physical education, music, dramatics, and science clubs, and the annual spring festival in Scammon Garden. A school Open House gave the pupils an opportunity to demonstrate classwork in their homerooms. In 1920, when elementary school tuition was raised to $225, and high school tuition to $275, the Parents' Association was relieved of the responsibility of underwriting extracurricular activities. Now included in the tuition were the social fee and all expenses for supplies, including textbooks. However, in 1924, the Association gave $100 to an "outside" person for special music classes in the elementary school and, in the following year, $500 to buy pictures for classrooms and corridors.

The Mothers' Prize of a twenty-dollar gold piece, first given in 1921, was bestowed annually on a girl of "refinement and courtesy, tolerance, cooperativeness, loyalty, and a moral and intellectual influence."

The History of the Laboratory Schools

IN SUMMARY

The twelve years from 1919 to 1931 were marked by Mr. Morrison's unit-and-mastery technique, which necessitated greater attention to the individual pupil. In the process of attaining mastery, deficiencies in learning, and especially in reading, were revealed and led to the addition of a remedial teacher to the elementary school staff as well as a psychologist to work in both schools. Diagnostic tests and recently devised standardized reading tests were used to locate deficiencies, and corrective work was instituted.

The extensive reports required from the teachers, plus other records, led to the establishment of a Records Office.

Because of the importance of reading in Mr. Morrison's scheme, a library for intermediate pupils was set up.

Ability grouping was tried and, after trial, discontinued.

The elementary school was limited to six years. Seventh-graders became sub-freshmen in the high school, and the whole period of schooling was now eleven years.

Methods of reporting to parents began a long history of scrutiny and change.

As for the teachers, they produced an astonishing number of textbooks, articles, monographs, book reviews, and services to education in general.

Were the principles of Mr. Dewey and Colonel Parker forgotten in the emphasis on mastery? Again, only seemingly. The students' freedom to move about and to question was never curtailed, although the urge to inquire, to investigate, and to challenge was not so impelling in the carefully organized unit work. Then, too, the appeal to the tactile sense, the use of the hand as well as the head, was temporarily in abeyance. As time went on, the best features of the Morrison technique were gradually winnowed out and combined with earlier ideas of worth and substance.

Times were changing. The Depression began to be felt, and there were other winds of change.

Seven

The Schools in the
Depression Years

1931–1940

On Black Friday, in October, 1929, the stock market
spiraled catastrophically downward. Within three years
the nation was gripped by the economic depression
which followed. By 1932, it had made itself deeply and
poignantly felt in the neighborhood of the Laboratory
Schools. When the banks in Chicago were closed in
March 1933, the students all knew that the economic
situation was very bad and did what they could to help.
The Hi-Y Club undertook to give twenty dollars a
month to the lunch committee of the Ray School Parent-
Teacher Association, so that boys and girls who had to
come to school without breakfast could have free food
in the morning and at noon. Members of the Girls'
Club gave twenty-five baskets of food to needy people.

At the elementary school faculty meeting in October,
1932, the principal announced that registration had
dropped from 460 in the previous year to 400. By
allowing parents to defer paying tuition and by providing more scholarships, the school was able to keep some

pupils who otherwise would have had to leave. The enrollment continued to drop in the Laboratory Schools through the following years, and the going was difficult, but somehow the Schools weathered the Depression.

GREEK LITERATURE FOR HIGH SCHOOL JUNIORS

In 1929, Robert Maynard Hutchins began his administration as president of the University, and in April, 1932, he and Mortimer Adler began a unique experiment—a lecture course in Greek literature for twenty-four members of the high school junior class. Gladys Campbell, a teacher in the high school English department who took part in the experiment, discussed it in an interview:

It was Mr. Hutchins' belief that students who were much younger than those who ordinarily enter the University freshman class were perfectly capable of doing college work. To demonstrate this, he asked for some students from U-High to try out the Great Books course, which was to be planned just like the one he had been carrying on with the University students. I had been sitting in on that for a year or so and had become acquainted with Mr. Hutchins and with the work, . . . and he asked me to help.

A group of students was asked to join in this project—a group whose teachers thought they were capable of doing more advanced work.

We tried out . . . three discussions in the spring of the first year. In the next year, students enrolled in the course and were given full credit for it. They met only two hours with Mr. Hutchins and Mr. Adler, and then met for another hour with another teacher and me. The students read the full text of all the Great Books, and the discussions, led by Mr. Hutchins and Mr. Adler, were remarkably good.

. . . At the end of the year, the examination consisted of two essays. Certain portions of books were taken, and the student was asked to write a full discussion of the excerpt that was given him, both in its own meaning and in its relationship to the entire work. These papers ran from forty to sixty pages, and some were remarkably well written.

. . . The whole plan came to an end because of the formation of the new college. It was considered that this course had proved to everybody who had anything to do with it that these better students could easily do the same kind of work that had been done by the older students in the University.

ACCENT ON CREATIVITY

Much creative writing and creative work were done in the Laboratory Schools, in the high school especially. Gladys Campbell, who had a creative writing class, reported in an interview:

> I think the most interesting work that I did in the University High School . . . was in the creative writing class. . . . The students were free to write anything they liked, although they were given stimulation from time to time in certain fields. I found that nearly all these students had an interest in more than one art, so I always did what I could to bring the arts together. Some students wrote stories and illustrated them. Some who wrote

A first-grade reading class uses pictures during reading instruction. Charts and pictures were used early in the reading program at the Laboratory Schools. Note the small class size and informal seating arrangement.

poems set them to music. . . . At the end of the year, the students were interested in preserving some of the best of their work, so they chose an editorial staff, and this staff, with the teacher's help, selected some of the best works of the year and published them in a little booklet. They called this *Fennelstalks* because Prometheus was supposed to have brought fire from heaven in a fennel stalk, and, of course, they were all interested in bringing fire from heaven.

Another high school teacher, Russell Thomas, wrote:

One special activity was the Senior dramatic organization in the High School (before it was transferred to the College), . . . which during my years as faculty sponsor changed its name to the Playfesters, and instituted an annual program, the Playfest, at which we always produced one play written by a student. What has delighted me is that a number of students who won recognition in the competition have continued to write and have won recognition either in drama or fiction.

There were other creative activities, as for example, the annual book fair, which received considerable attention since it was almost completely student-managed; the puppet show presented by the Art Club at the same fair; the display of rare books relating to drama which the Playfesters presented; and the letters from foreign countries shown by the International Correspondence Club.

The Schools in the Depression Years

In 1936, the high school was one of thirty experimental secondary schools and two hundred and fifty colleges selected from all over the United States for an eight-year cooperative study sponsored by the Progressive Education Association. The aims of the experiment were to effect changes in the direction of greater continuity of learning, better integration of subject matter, more vital instruction and release of creative energies, and better adjustment to individual capacities.

The plan provided for an eight-year period, beginning in 1936, during which the schools involved would experiment with any desired type of tests or curriculum. Reconstruction of the secondary school curriculum was encouraged. The two hundred and fifty designated colleges agreed to accept the students from the cooperating schools without the usual entrance requirements. The approval of the principal, plus a considerable body of tests and personal information gathered during the students' high school years, took the place of those requirements.

The study had two major purposes: (1) to establish a relationship between school and college that would permit and encourage reconstruction in the secondary school, and (2) to learn, through exploration and experimentation, how high schools in the United States could serve youth more effectively.

The results of the study were not only highly encouraging but also of far-reaching significance. Graduates of the thirty high schools were found to be as ready for college work as those who had studied under the conventional curriculum. Moreover, the more revisions a school had made in its curriculum, the higher the standing of its students when compared with students of equal ability from other high schools.

THE NEW COLLEGE

During the year 1932–33, the new College of the University of Chicago began to take form, and steps were taken to bring it into a close working relationship with the University High School. A high school teacher explained the basis for this relationship:

> The fact that students in University High School were taking college work was not a new thing. They had been taking some college courses for some time. For a couple of years, I gave the College English course and followed the plan that was outlined for the work of the English department across campus.

To qualify for courses in the College, a student had to have fifteen credits as well as a high general standing.

Early in 1933, the Board of Trustees approved a recommendation of the University Senate to incorporate the last two years of the high school into the program of the college. The College faculty and the teachers of high school seniors forthwith set about preparing the curriculum. The seniors would get double credit in their college courses because such courses contributed to the requirements for both the high school diploma and the college certificate. The plan attracted national attention, since for many years there had been widespread discussion on how to achieve a smooth transition from high school to college.

The new curriculum was initiated at the beginning

The Schools in the Depression Years

of the 1933–34 school year. For each student in the junior and senior classes, the decision had to be made whether he would graduate under the old or the new requirements. Students of outstanding ability in particular fields were allowed to begin college work in those fields in their senior year, unless their parents preferred otherwise. According to *The New Curriculum in the High School,* a descriptive circular issued in April, 1933:

> The new plan stresses thoroughness of work rather than encyclopedic completeness. Under the plan, greater mastery of essential tools of language and mathematics is stressed as well as a broader view of the social and natural environment.

Individual achievement was recognized in many ways. In English, for example, if by the end of his sophomore year a student could demonstrate that he had reached a level of maturity in oral and written language beyond that reached by students in their senior year, he was not required to continue formal study of English expression. Then, too, the new plan included a feature called "special responsibilities." All students whom the faculty considered to be capable of planning, and being responsible for, their own time were permitted to come and go as they saw fit as long as they maintained a high scholastic record.

The University's four-year College came into full operation in the autumn of 1938, after several years of curriculum planning and integration of courses. The last two years of high school were combined with the first two years of college. A separate faculty was organized, to which several teachers of University High School junior and senior classes were transferred. Separate quarters were provided in 1939 at 5810 Woodlawn Avenue, but since there was not enough space for all the classes, science, foreign languages, and mathematics were taught in Belfield Hall. Neither were there adequate library facilities, so the high school library had to serve both the high school and the College.

In 1937–38, another year was added to the high school by reinstating the eighth grade, and the term "sub-freshman" was dropped. The high school was now composed of the seventh and eighth grades and the freshman and sophomore years. More time could therefore be given to English and social studies. Three years were to be used for the regular course in English. The fourth year was added so that some students could have extra help and others could do creative writing.

The shift of high school juniors and seniors to the College was not accomplished without extra-curricular problems. For example, high school publications had to be taken over by groups two years younger and without previous experience. The tenth-grade class, whose average age was fourteen, was the oldest group, and they fulfilled their new obligations creditably. Girls' Club teas and various money-collecting drives also had to be shouldered by a younger group. Also, the constitutions of the various school organizations had to be reorganized. The Boys' Club tried a dual board, but this did not work, since some boys were unequal to the responsibilities entailed. Athletic competition was likewise affected, especially inter-school games. High school students had to compete against older and more mature students from other schools. A modified system of awards had to be devised, and some high school awards were taken over by the College.

These and many other problems had to be solved,

but, on the other hand, the new program brought many compensations. For the students who were able and responsible, it was both stimulating and satisfying.

THE GRADING SYSTEM AND THE GUIDANCE PROGRAM

Certain parts of the Laboratory Schools program were changed many times and went through many phases. The grading system, previously mentioned, was one; the guidance program was another.

The earlier discussion of the system of reporting pupils' progress to parents explained various changes in the system, up to and including the use of letters to parents in the high school and of check lists in the elementary school. In 1936–37, letter grades—A, B, C, D—were re-instituted in the high school. An executive committee decided on the exact meaning of each letter, and the faculty began using the system the following year. In the elementary school, a second type of check list replaced the first.

In like manner, the guidance program went through several changes between 1931 and 1940. For many years the program had been in the hands of the assistant principal, but in 1934, the responsibility was given to the staff psychologist, who set up a new program. Twenty teachers were organized into five committees and a certain number of committee members assigned to each class as advisers. A student had the same adviser in his sub-freshman and freshman years, then changed to another for his sophomore, junior, and senior years. The purpose of distributing the students among many advisers was to make sure each student had close personal attention, guidance, and counseling throughout his high school years.

The History of the Laboratory Schools

Actually the need for this new program had become increasingly apparent. When the assistant principal was the only student adviser, he had not been able to give much time to individual students. But the high school faculty felt a student's problems, both educational and personal, were highly important to his academic progress, and for this reason a good guidance program was essential.

To help the faculty advisers, a program of training was set up in 1934–35 and continued for two years. The plan had its praiseworthy points. However, consensus of opinion among so many advisers was difficult to achieve; the means of counseling were diverse; and definitions of personality adjustment were many. The staff psychologist resigned, and the guidance program reverted to the principal and assistant principal.

Two years later, another plan was tried. Three teachers were relieved of one class apiece to give them time for individual counseling on educational and personal problems. These three carried on for another two years until the autumn of 1940, when the Laboratory Schools again had a staff psychologist.

Thus the problem of guidance, though never satisfactorily solved, was never sloughed off. If one solution did not work, another was tried—a different approach from another angle—and the experiments went on.

THE NURSERY SCHOOL

In this semi-chronological history of the Laboratory Schools it is difficult to determine in which period to place the nursery school. But it was in the decade of the 1930's that the school became formally organized and also when it was taken over by the University's School of Education.

The University Co-operative Nursery really had its beginning, in an informal way, back in 1916. A small group of women, under the leadership of Mrs. Frank R. Lillie, worked out a plan whereby each took turns caring for the children of all the mothers in the group. For the first three months, the children met daily out of doors, in Scammon Garden. When winter came, a place had to be found for indoor as well as outdoor play, so the mothers got permission to use the women's gymnasium in Lexington Hall, with the University providing heat, light, and janitor service. This arrangement went on until 1923, when the University needed Lexington Hall for other purposes. At that time a generous gift from Mrs. Lillie, plus the fund-raising efforts of members of the group, made it possible to purchase a house at 5750 Woodlawn Avenue.

In the 1920's, the nursery school movement was just getting started. The University Co-operative Nursery School, incorporated in 1923, was not the first in the country, but, according to one of its members, it was one of the first to have its own building. Each mother gave a half or a whole day of service to the school, and payment for this work was credited to her account. Mothers who were employed, and therefore could not serve, paid tuition.

The mothers were eager and enthusiastic. The nursery school was their project, and they worked very hard to keep it functioning. Seeking the best advice they could get, they consulted Lydia Roberts, chairman of the University's Department of Home Economics, on matters of nutrition related to the children's daily lunches, and Alice Temple, head of the Kindergarten Department, for counsel on other matters.

When the school went into its new building, a professional teacher was acquired, but the mothers continued to serve half days. Before long, the enrollment had increased, more teachers were added, and more room was needed.

In 1929, the three-story building at 5740 Woodlawn Avenue was purchased through the generosity of the University and of Dr. Walter H. O. Hoffmann, a pediatrician on the staff of Presbyterian Hospital. It was specified that the newly acquired building be used jointly by the nursery school and by the Department of Home Economics and Household Administration for research in child care and development.

Miss Roberts was much interested in working with Dr. Hoffmann on problems of health and nutrition. This was an era of important advances in child immunization, in development of anti-toxins, and in control of contagion, and Dr. Hoffmann and Miss Roberts cooperated in providing the mothers with information concerning these and other new developments in child health. Miss Roberts also carried on studies of the role of vitamins, just recently discovered, in health. Dr. Hoffmann examined the children each day for colds or communicable diseases. Because all this research was of great interest to the mothers, the program became one of parent education. Thus the nursery school was a laboratory as well, and students, too, carried on studies in health and nutrition there.

The opportunities for psychological work afforded by the nursery school were not utilized until psychologist Helen L. Koch came in 1929. She accepted a place on the nursery school board with the understanding that her students could use the school for observation. At the same time, she undertook to educate the staff in child care and in nursery school techniques. She conducted parent study groups on topics in which there was widespread interest during the late 1920's and early 1930's: the intelligence quotient, early psychoanalysis, and mental hygiene. These groups were addressed by members of the University faculty prominent in such fields as sociology, human development, psychology, and home economics.

In 1933, the nursery school board decided to formalize the organization and appointed Dr. Koch director. Parents continued to serve, but since fees were small, the school had its financial problems, especially during the Depression. Almost all the nursery schools in the nation had to close, and the board, in desperation, was ready to give the school to the University. However, the University wanted the fees raised, and the school's old clientele would not consent to this. So, with the help of many faculty members and the hard work of the mothers, the school somehow managed to survive.

Eventually the University Co-operative Nursery School was taken over by the School of Education and renamed the University of Chicago Nursery School. This was in 1938. Its administration of the school was placed in the hands of the Child Development Committee, and it became an integral part of the Laboratory Schools system, under the Board of Pre-Collegiate Education.

During World War II, the nursery school made a vital contribution. War nurseries had sprung up in all areas, and trained teachers were not available. Dr. Koch gave in-service teacher training courses and supervised the practice teaching of those in training. A film made at the school to illustrate nursery practices had wide circulation—even in England, where day nurseries were being set up but without a pattern to follow. In spite of the mobility of the staff and shortages of every kind, the nursery school kept a superior group of teachers.

When the war was over, the school again became a laboratory for research and studies. A great variety of questions was raised. What playground equipment was appropriate for nursery-age children? How could the problem of contagious diseases, especially colds, be handled? What to do about children who would not eat? Studies were made on these and other problems— techniques of getting a child to sleep at naptime, the need for a mid-morning snack, tensions in children, the unsocial child, the child's concept of self, the sex role of the child, and techniques of building confidence.

The nursery school served many University departments. Instructors in pediatrics sent interns to observe the children. From psychology came students who did basic work on the learning curve; from sociology, students interested in group structure. The school also provided practice teaching for students from other nearby colleges and universities.

Despite all these services and uses, the school still lacked funds. By 1955, its buildings were in sad need of repair. Janitorial service had been inadequate, and the University had not allotted necessary funds for upkeep. The two houses were so run down that the school might have to close if funds were not available to rehabilitate them. Hence a study was made of its functions and purposes—and as a result $25,000 was allocated for the necessary rehabilitation. The buildings

A kindergarten building project shows a mail truck and locomotive. The children in the foreground are busily building crossing gates for safety instruction. On the wall is an early form of experience chart used in reading instruction.

were refurbished, inside and out; new equipment was bought; and the school put in good order. In the years that followed, the departments of Psychology, Psychiatry, Human Development, and Education all carried on study, observation, and research there.

Some interesting statistics have been compiled on the uses made of the nursery school in research projects for doctoral dissertations and Master's theses. Between 1949 and 1955, seven formal research projects leading to Ph.D. degrees were carried on by students in education, human development, and psychology, and five by students working for M.A.'s in home economics, education, and human development. The Department of Nursing Education had sent graduate students specializing in pediatric nursing to gain experience in the nursery school. In one year no fewer than fifty-six persons used it for research.

The University of Chicago Nursery School, then, has been not only an excellent nursery school—a model to which other nursery school teachers have gone for source material and special observation. It has also been a center for research and study, the results of which have been spread widely through published articles and addresses given by the staff, through service to preschool organizations, through the influence of principals and teachers trained in the school who took positions elsewhere, and through parents and visitors. Experimentation has continued to this day and will undoubtedly increase as more young children are involved in programs such as Project Head Start. Recent research has focused on reading, mathematics, concepts of animal life, spoken Russian, and community structure, and a socio-emotional rating scale is in the process of being perfected. Moreover, the parents are kept abreast of the various experiments so that they may be constantly aware of the direction in which the education of the nursery child is moving.

THE LABORATORY SCHOOLS KINDERGARTEN

As a background for the history of the Laboratory Schools kindergarten, it is of interest to review the beginnings of the kindergarten movement in America, more than a century ago.

The Froebel kindergarten was introduced into the United States in 1855 by Mrs. Carl Schurz, who began one for her own children and children of other German families in Watertown, Wisconsin. However, credit for the real spread of the kindergarten idea must go to Elizabeth Peabody of Boston, who in 1860 enthusiastically advocated this form of pre-school education.

The first kindergartens were either private or organized by church or settlement groups. The teaching was formalized and detailed, following a day-by-day plan which was so explicit that teachers could be quickly trained. It was based entirely on the philosophy of Froebel, which was symbolized by "gifts" with mystical connotations and "occupations" related to the gifts. The gifts were small-sized objects such as balls an inch and a half in diameter, and one-inch cubes. Rarely was a child allowed to play freely with these materials. What he did with them was dictated by the teacher in accordance with definite developmental steps. To digress from the prescribed order of the steps was not tolerated by the devoted followers of Froebel.

The kindergarten movement was given strong impetus at the 1876 Exposition in Philadelphia and later at the 1893 Columbian Exposition in Chicago, where demonstration kindergartens were held. In Chicago, the kindergarten was in operation during the entire six months of the Exposition and was one of the most popular exhibits of the Fair.

Between 1890 and 1900, criticisms of the Froebel method began to be heard. The play materials were too small for children's fingers, said critics, and the closely supervised artwork was far too formal. Even the games and songs were inappropriate. The critics held that education should be a "process of development rather than a process of instruction," that "the child's creative activity must be the main factor in his education," and that "his present interests and needs rather than the demands of the future should determine the material and methods to be employed." (Nina Van de Walker, *The Kindergarten in American Education*, page 245.)

Across the country kindergarten teachers split up into conservative and liberal factions. Indeed, the division was so sharp that a committee of nineteen of the International Kindergarten Union was appointed to study and evaluate the claims of each side. The committee, after working earnestly for several years, finally came out with a majority report in favor of modern, liberal procedures.

In Mr. Dewey's kindergarten, which opened in 1898, there was no question about the path to be followed; it was the path he himself had marked out so clearly in his educational philosophy. The children were to start with familiar experiences—activities that went on in every child's home. For example, *Teacher Reports* for 1898–99, the year the kindergarten was established, describes the activities as follows:

The Schools in the Depression Years

To October 28. The general topic for the quarter was the family and the home. . . . The games were based on . . . the duties of the home. The construction work was based on things which they felt the need of in their school home. They were told stories and worked out their ideas in clay and in color. . . .

To November 11. The children made a large playhouse from a box. This was papered and painted and nailed together. The children decided on the number of rooms that would be needed, and each child made a house of a smaller box. This was taken home. They dug earth in the garden to fill the window garden box in school. They made jelly for Thanksgiving.

To November 23. Preparations for Thanksgiving. Corn pone baked. Found out where corn comes from. This was dramatized. Made dishes of pasteboard to hold candy for souvenirs. For Thanksgiving dinner, there was cocoa which the children made, and jelly and marmalade which they had made.

To December 2. Finishing playhouse. Kitchen stove made of tin. Tin dipper and pans. Made a bed of wood and a cradle of manila paper. A bureau with drawers. A pedestal of a spool.

To January 13. Subject: Heating homes. Children made stoves using cubes 2 x 2 inches. Used thread boxes for construction.

To January 27. Cooked rice. Made beds from cigar boxes, made blankets for beds.

To February 3. Curtains made for old-fashioned bed, also sheets, pillowcases, and blankets.

To February 17. Visited dry goods store. Mother buying . . . dramatized. The store was built of blocks and children acted as clerks, cash boys, floorwalker, . . . cable car conductors. Pasted cloth dresses on paper dolls. Made mittens, hoods, and overshoes of different colored paper.

To April 28. Housecleaning. Made pails of heavy manila paper, scrub brushes with bristles of rope, dust pan and broom of soft tin. Cooked farina.

In the *Reports* for the following year, 1899–1900, the heading *Kindergarten* was replaced by *Sub-Primary, Groups I and II.* These groups were evidently made up of older and younger children, perhaps four- and five-year-olds. The teacher continued to use some small-sized articles, such as cigar boxes and matchboxes for playhouse furniture, but the children had larger equipment, too. They washed clothes with real washboards, painted a large windowbox, and made streetcars with chairs. There was also much cooking. The youngsters made cornmeal mush and jelly, popped corn, and cooked apricots. They went on outings to the Field Museum and to Washington Park. They took a bus trip to Jackson Park and got polliwogs for their aquarium.

Even these few examples show how faithfully Mr. Dewey's principles were practiced in his kindergarten. There was no break between a child's experiences in his own home and those in the school. He began with such simple, familiar activities as cooking, sewing, drawing, coloring, sawing, nailing, and modeling. He listened to stories and dramatized incidents from them, sang songs, played vigorously with other children, and went on trips and observed nature.

He lived in the present and learned to be part of a social group. His curiosity aroused, he was challenged to find his own ways of constructing, dramatizing, painting, modeling. There was no need for false incentives, no need for prizes. Learning was interesting, challenging, and happy.

After June, 1900, no more kindergarten reports were issued by Mr. Dewey's teachers; at least none are now available. It was in 1900, however, that a new kindergarten teacher, Anne Allen, came to the school. Strongly influenced by Mr. Dewey's ideas, she broke with Froebel's gifts and occupations and made the kindergarten activities natural and of the child's interest. Instead of the small wooden cubes, she had large blocks made, which the children could use to build playhouses or stores or schools—all big enough for them to play in. Gone was Froebel's circle of little chairs. Miss Allen had a rug laid on the floor, so the children could sit on it beside her chair, just as they would in their own homes. She brought in play materials not found in Froebel kindergartens—dolls, housekeeping utensils, wagons, and doll buggies. Instead of following a fixed plan, the children helped plan their own activities.

The teachers who succeeded Anne Allen continued to practice Mr. Dewey's ideas. One of them, Olga Adams, who taught in the Laboratory Schools for many years vividly stated her recollections:

> The teachers who preceded me stressed, with great effectiveness, child participation in the planning of group activities and the development of independent thinking and decision-making.

One of my predecessors had a project on the city. The children planned and built a miniature city of blocks on the floor of the kindergarten room. This portrayed their own community, and much of the information for it was gained through walks around the neighborhood. I was much impressed by their interest, the challenge to their thinking, and the amount of information and understanding they gained from this project.

Each spring through all the years I was in the kindergarten, a setting hen, with the resulting family of chicks, was a thrilling experience for the children. I inherited the cage from former teachers.

Perhaps my most distinct contribution to the kindergarten was an abundance of animal life— always the aquarium with fish, snails, and tadpoles in season, the terrarium with turtles, a toad or frog, a garter snake, a rabbit which had the freedom of the room, visiting dogs and cats, a skunk for one season, and even a pig for a three-day visit. The fall brought cocoons and the spring, moths. I felt that city children needed this close association with, and responsibility for, as great a variety of animals as could be cared for properly in the kindergarten room.

The earliest kindergartens were never a part of the public school system and had no connection with later work in the primary grades. Then, though public schools in some states began to have kindergartens, there was still a sharp distinction between what was taught there and what was taught in first grade. But Alice Temple, of the School of Education faculty, saw kindergarten and first grade as a consecutive experience.

Her contribution to education was the unification of the kindergarten and primary grades.

The Laboratory Schools kindergarten teachers have continued to carry out Mr. Dewey's ideas. True, the equipment has changed. The dolls are made of plastic and rubber instead of bisque and china, the playhouse furnishings have gone modern, and corrugated paper boxes are used along with blocks for construction. There is a greater variety of playground equipment— and of picture books, too. Now the children have maps and globes and even a set of reference books.

LABORATORIES IN NAME ONLY

In the early 1930's, the tie between the University and the Laboratory Schools was loosening—in both an organizational and an educational sense. The Laboratory Schools were no longer a center for experimentation, for trying out new ideas. The departments of the College and University which were concerned with teaching methods no longer used the schools for the purpose implied in their name—that is, as laboratories. Of course, individual students still carried on research there, but what had been a very close relationship for thirty years was gradually diminishing. Not until 1953 were steps taken to re-establish it. In that year, Harold B. Dunkel, the University's Director of Pre-Collegiate Education, was asked to re-explore relations between the schools and the University. As a result, in 1954, the elementary school was used by the Education Department for training elementary school teachers. In 1958, the schools were assigned as laboratories to the Graduate School of Education.

In the summer of 1938, Mr. Judd retired and was

succeeded by Ralph W. Tyler, who became chairman of the Department of Education in the University's Division of Social Sciences. Mr. Tyler had come to Chicago from Ohio State University, where he had been professor of education and research associate in the Bureau of Educational Research. Mr. William C. Reavis, formerly principal of the high school, was superintendent of the Laboratory Schools from 1938 to 1940.

Eight

Pre-War Progress
and Wartime Changes
1940–1944

A new superintendent came to the Laboratory Schools in 1940—Stephen M. Corey, who had been chairman of the Department of Educational Methods at the University of Wisconsin, as well as assistant dean of the Graduate School and professor of education. His four years as superintendent were marked by more democratic procedures, by the formation of teacher committees and discussion groups, by an increase in professional leadership among the teachers, and by an emphasis on child study and child development research.

THE LABORATORY SCHOOL COUNCIL

Among the first new organizations set up by Mr. Corey was the Laboratory Schools Council. Composed of the superintendent, the two principals, the dean of boys and dean of girls, and four teachers chosen at large from the combined faculties, the Council was formed to discuss school problems, decide what should be done about them, and recommend action to the faculty. In 1943, it was enlarged to include another teacher, elected by the faculty, and, some months later, three parents from the elementary school and three from the high school, all elected by the Parents' Association.

In the autumn of 1941, shortly before Pearl Harbor, three major topics were considered by the Council: the decrease in high school enrollment, the publication of a Laboratory School bulletin to keep parents and friends up to date on the schools' activities, and the preparation of a list of the responsibilities expected of a Laboratory School teacher in addition to effective teaching.

The high school enrollment had been dropping ever since the Depression. The Council, after discussing the problem at length, recommended that the dean of girls go to neighboring high schools, tell the students about the Laboratory Schools, and invite visitors. The plan, though simple, was highly successful. Inquiries began to flow in, and more and more students applied for admission to University High School. In the next two years, the enrollment increased by seventy students. Interestingly enough, that particular problem has never arisen again.

The purpose of the proposed Laboratory Schools bulletin, the second topic on the Council's agenda, was partly to publicize the schools, but partly also to survey their program and reveal strong and weak points. Following full discussion, steps were taken to prepare and publish such a bulletin.

On the third topic, faculty responsibilities, Mr. Corey drafted a memorandum setting forth what he considered to be the avenues of professional leadership open to Laboratory Schools teachers. The list was impressive: leadership in some extra-school activity, child development research, curriculum materials research, development of tests and monographs based on careful research, consultative services to schools and other agencies concerned with educational problems, active participation in national, state, and local educational organizations, and addresses before professional and lay groups. The Council discussed the memorandum and submitted it to the faculty.

NEW VIGOR IN THE ELEMENTARY SCHOOL

In the elementary school, after the intensive work during Mr. Morrison's regime in the 1920's and 1930's, there had been a breathing spell for a few years. Then, under the stimulation of the new director, the school again became a center of professional leadership and influence. The *Staff Newsletter,* a monthly mimeographed sheet inaugurated in October, 1941, reported on the Council's discussions, informed teachers about one another's professional activities, and served as a medium of exchange for new educational ideas. Here each month the many and varied activities of the faculty were listed—the book reviews and articles written, the lectures given, the research under way, the "round tables" conducted, the demonstration lessons presented, the graduate work undertaken, the University College courses taught, and the books published. So extensive were these activities that the third issue of the *Newsletter* contained an apologetic note, saying that the list was too long to print in its entirety.

The History of the Laboratory Schools

The school year 1942–43 was notable for more professional activities among the faculty members than ever before: 73 articles and three books and monographs published; 33 graduate courses taken; 21 research projects completed; 53 state, local, and national committee offices held; 138 addresses given; and 39 major consultative services provided. There was no question but that the Schools were continuing to maintain their influence in the educational world.

At this time, there was a tremendous surge of interest, the country over, in the physical and psychological development of children. To acquaint the Laboratory Schools teachers with past studies and current research in this comparatively new field, members of the University's School of Education gave lectures and led discussions, and the school psychologist conducted a child study seminar.

Teachers were urged to undertake research projects on some phase of child development, not only for their own professional growth but for the information they might gain and share. Every Saturday morning they met to report their research activities. The titles of some of their studies indicate the breadth of their interests and inquiries: "Vocabulary Growth in Superior Second-Grade Children," "Evaluation of the Effectiveness of a Combined English-Social Studies Program as a Means of Teaching Desirable Attitudes," "Diagnostic Tests: Basic Concepts of Common and Decimal Fractions," "Effectiveness of Sketching as a Medium of Expression for Third-Grade Children," "Development of an Interest Inventory for Middle-Grade Children," "Color

A primary class builds a city. In addition to ideas in social stud-ies, reading and mathematics played a large part in this activity. Ideas about zoning and city growth patterns become obvious.

The History of the Laboratory Schools

Choices Among Second-Grade Children in a Free Situation," and "Evaluation of the Effectiveness of a Seventh- and Eighth-Grade Unified Arts Program."

In addition to this child study research, the elementary school teachers were taking a good look at the curriculum, with the idea of recommending needed changes. One committee scrutinized the curriculum in history and geography, based on Mr. Morrison's unit outline and unchanged for more than fifteen years. Now, however, national educational groups were urging that history and geography be known as social studies and taught as one subject. The committee therefore went to work on a new social studies curriculum for grades one through six, which, with minor changes and adaptations from time to time, was used for several years. Other curriculum committees pursued the same course, reflecting a marked and widespread trend toward teacher participation in curriculum making as well as in school decisions generally.

THE SCHOOLS IN WORLD WAR II

December 7, 1941, the day that changed the course of world history, wrought significant changes in the Laboratory Schools. In March, 1942, the Navy took over Sunny and Bartlett gymnasiums to house a thousand men in training, and also Jackman Field. One of the largest navy signal corps schools in the country was installed on the second and third floors of the west end of Belfield Hall. Boys went back to Gym Temp for their physical education, and girls used Ida Noyes pool for swimming and for locker rooms.

A Red Cross paper drive was launched, and the U-Hi chapter of the Junior Red Cross spent its funds on materials for other Red Cross projects. By April, the faculty began making plans for air-raid drills. To avoid danger from flying glass, shelters had to be located in coat rooms and inner corridors where there were no windows. In shop classes high school boys and girls made games for the navy trainees in Sunny Gymnasium, and elementary school children collected books and magazines for the men to read.

The high school principal, Mr. Paul B. Jacobsen, was asked to organize and direct the training program for radio operators which the University was carrying on for the Navy. The elementary school principal, Harry O. Gillet, was made chairman of a draft board. One of the teachers was granted full-time leave to serve as chief of typewriting on the radio training project, and two others were involved in the civilian pilot training program. Six faculty members left to go into military service.

A project worked out in World War I was repeated during World War II. In the summer of 1942, six high school boys were placed on farms to give needed help during the manpower shortage. In 1943, there were sixteen high school farm workers.

War activities mounted as time went on. A book drive was held. A course in first aid was given. War stamp sales reached $1,600 by April, 1943. The Junior Red Cross collected pictures, cartoons, and crossword puzzles and made scrapbooks for servicemen. By the autumn of 1943, the Navy had taken over another room in Belfield Hall, plus the auditorium in Judd Hall. One of the teachers conducted a program of training for child-care aides who would serve in nurseries for the working mothers.

The question of admitting Negro pupils to the Laboratory Schools had arisen from time to time over the years, and on each occasion the administration had decided not to do so, even though pupils of Oriental extraction were accepted. In 1942, some of the parents raised the question once more. Their views were stated in a letter from Mrs. Louis Gottschalk to Mr. Corey on December 3:

> Since we are engaged in a war in which our enemies are using the doctrine of racism as one of their principal weapons to enslave the world, we believe it important to demonstrate in our institutions and personal conduct that we believe in the opposite principle of equal opportunity for all people irrespective of race, color, and creed. . . .
>
> By admitting qualified Negro pupils to the Laboratory School, we will make it possible for our children to experience the meaning of democratic citizenship which we now deny them.

Three parents submitted this statement of beliefs to the principal of the elementary school and asked for his reaction to it. He replied that he himself was not opposed, but he wondered how the parents felt about it. The three—Mrs. Gottschalk, Mrs. Alex Elson, and Mrs. Leon Despres—discussed the matter informally with other parents, giving each one full opportunity to express his feelings. They then drew up a petition in favor of admitting Negroes and circulated it among 261 families of Laboratory Schools pupils. The result was that 209 families signed the petition. Among the 52 who did not sign, the objection expressed most frequently had to do with the social adjustment within the school community. How would Negro families fit in at picnics, outings, and teas? Would they be comfortable? Would Negro children be happy in the Laboratory Schools?

When Mr. Corey received the petition, he brought the matter before the Laboratory Schools Council. The Council firmly agreed that "Negro children should be admitted to the Schools as soon as this could be done with maximum benefit to all concerned."

How could integration be best accomplished? That was the next question. In the spring of 1943, it was decided to admit Negro children to the kindergarten and thereafter to the elementary grades, and the first Negro pupils were enrolled the following fall. As far as can be ascertained, the Laboratory Schools were the first private schools in Chicago to admit Negroes. A year later Francis Parker School also opened its doors to Negro children.

While the move was parent-initiated and parent-organized, the teachers, too, played an important role. In the elementary school they tried to anticipate any problems that might arise as a result of the new policy and discussed these frankly with their pupils. High school teachers took similar steps. In February, 1943, a tenth-grade social studies class which had been studying racial discrimination exchanged visits with a group of students from DuSable High School, an all-Negro school, and participated in joint discussions on the problems of minority groups. The University High School social studies teacher commented: "It was really an illuminating experience for my students. I don't think anything I taught them that year was as valuable."

THE UNIFIED ARTS PROGRAM

In spite of the many wartime activities, with their heavy demands on the staff's time and energy, a number of new experimental projects were launched during this period. A new unified arts program was initiated, with a six-week try-out in the eighth grade, for the purpose of helping students to integrate their knowledge and see relationships in art, shop, dramatics, music, home arts, and publications. The eighth-grade class was divided into groups concerned with each of these areas, but all students moved from one group to another as they planned and carried out projects under the guidance of teachers in art, home economics, shop, printing, and typewriting. The program was broadened to include seventh-graders and continues to this day. Cutting across subject-matter boundaries, it enables students to see relationships among many different kinds of art activity, thus challenging and stimulating their creative efforts.

PUPIL PUBLICATIONS

The High School had had a variety of publications from its earliest days, but the elementary grades had had none for many years—not since the teacher of printing had retired. Now, however, the publishing of a newspaper became part of the seventh- and eighth-grade typewriting program. The *7th Grade Brainstorm* came first, in 1941, and from then on, for the next ten years, the seventh and eighth grades produced variously named, typed, and duplicated "newspapers" of three to six pages. The elementary grades soon followed suit with the *Elementary News,* which contained writing from all the grades. The editorial board included eight pupils, from grades three through six, and four faculty members. This publication continued for only a short time, but in succeeding years individual grades produced their own newspapers.

SUMMER SCHOOL

In 1940, both schools held a five-week summer session in which teachers tried out new and important ideas that could be incorporated into the regular year's work. The elementary school offered a program of enrichment —art, music, play and games, dramatics, swimming, social studies, and a library period for free reading— that gave teachers a chance to experiment with new materials and correlate various kinds of subject matter. Grade levels were ignored, and children from two and sometimes three age groups worked together happily and productively.

In the high school summer session, teachers experimented with a "core" curriculum. Social studies and English were combined to give life and pertinence to the problems studied. In the next two years, this core curriculum was carried into the seventh and eighth grades, with teachers of English and social studies working together.

With a few interruptions, the summer sessions have been continued to the present time. They have been of real value, not only to the teachers and students but to countless visiting observers who have carried away with them many useful ideas and suggestions for their own classroom work.

A NEW TEACHER IS ADDED TO THE FACULTY

It was in the early 1940's that the elementary school teachers sent out a call for help on behalf of pupils with speech difficulties—more help than they themselves were equipped to give. Acting on a proposal by the School Council, Joseph Wepman, director of the speech clinic at the University Clinics, conducted a "speech survey" of all the pupils. When he discovered a prevailing carelessness in speech, throughout the grades, he recommended that the children be given formal training in enunciation. Since Dr. Wepman also suggested that a specialist in the speech arts be added to the faculty, a teacher of dramatics and speech was forthwith appointed.

LEADERSHIP IN TRANSITION

In 1944, the Schools lost their superintendent and both their principals. In January, the University asked Mr. Corey to take a six months' leave of absence in order to act as educational adviser to the Encyclopaedia Britannica Corporation, which had just come under the University's direction. The high school principal, Mr. Jacobsen, was to devote his full time to administering certain war projects, and the elementary school principal, Mr. Gillet, was scheduled for retirement.

When Mr. Gillet retired in June, 1944, he had completed forty-three years in the Laboratory Schools. He had taught under Mr. Dewey and Colonel Parker. He had worked closely with the parents and knew every child in the elementary school, having interviewed and admitted all new applicants except the kindergarteners.

In recognition of his years of devoted service, parents, teachers, and children contributed well over six thousand dollars to a scholarship fund for elementary school pupils—the Helen C. and Harry O. Gillet Scholarship Fund, honoring both him and his wife. Each year Mr. Gillet met with a committee to choose the children who would receive financial help from the scholarship fund. He believed that the young recipients should be chosen on the basis of their industry, good citizenship, and ability to profit from the school program. Sometimes as many as five and six children were given partial scholarships, sometimes only one or two.

The teachers, for their part, wished to honor Mr. Gillet in a special way. The flagpole outside the north entrance to Blaine Hall, which represents their contribution, has a plate at its base bearing his name and years of service.

Nine

Achieving Unity

1944–1957

Why should there be two Laboratory Schools? Why not a single school, from kindergarten through high school? Since a new director had to be appointed, why not break with administrative tradition now, in 1944? The idea seemed a sound one to those concerned with the functioning of the Schools. It was decided that the director would be both superintendent and principal, would head the combined schools, and would administer their program. His major task, in cooperation with the faculty, would be to form a single school from two essentially separate ones.

In the spring of 1944, a small committee, consisting of two faculty members and a representative of the Parents' Association, met with Mr. Tyler to consider possible candidates. Eventually they chose Warren Crocker Seyfert, principal of the Browne and Nichols Country Day School at Cambridge, Massachusetts, and former professor of education in the Harvard University Graduate School. In order that the new director might have a clear field, the positions of high school and elementary school principal were not filled, and the positions of dean of boys and dean of girls were abolished.

PLANNING WEEK

One of the first of Mr. Seyfert's innovations was Planning Week, the week preceding the opening of school. It was a busy time, devoted to general faculty meetings, committee meetings, orientation of new teachers, and schedule-making. Since there was now to be one school instead of two, new faculty committees had to be appointed to consider problems common to both elementary and high school programs. Thus the process of welding the two schools together was begun.

To symbolize that unification, the name was changed from plural to singular: the Laboratory School. The elementary grades were called the lower school and the high school the upper school, although "U-Hi" continued to be used by many students. By the end of the decade, however, the old names were restored: Laboratory *Schools,* University High School, and University Elementary School.

ACHIEVING UNITY

Mr. Seyfert, a firm believer in the democratic process, appointed a large number of committees, including a policy committee, to consider, discuss, and resolve problems of small groups and of concern to the school as a whole. The Laboratory Schools Council, begun by Mr. Corey, was continued, and later the "little faculties" were formed.

Assemblies, important in Mr. Dewey's and Colonel Parker's programs, were equally important forty years afterward, and all-school assemblies now became a hoped-for means of creating a spirit of unity. However, since the school had an enrollment of approximately seven hundred students, there was no hall large enough to accommodate all of them. Assemblies for the lower school were held in Sunny Gymnasium, and the upper school continued to gather in Mandel Hall. Finally, in 1946, at Thanksgivingtime, an all-school assembly was held in Rockefeller Chapel. The Christmas exercises also took place there, and the custom continued for many years.

POSTWAR CHANGES

The war ended in 1945, and Sunny Gymnasium, Jackman Field, and the Belfield rooms which had been used by the Navy were returned to the school. But not for long. Two years later the school had to give up two rooms in Belfield to three new University institutes: nuclear studies, studies of metals, and radio biology. New rooms at the east end of Belfield therefore had to be extensively remodeled to accommodate high school shop equipment as well as home economics and art classes.

SOCIAL LIFE IN THE SCHOOL

Through the years the problem of working out a truly educative social life in the University High School had continued to preoccupy its staff. After the war, a general trend toward disorganized, disruptive gatherings, both at home and at school, impressed teachers and parents alike with the need for a balanced social program for the entire school. No policy had ever been set up for its social activities; nor had the school's social goals been fully interpreted to parents so that home and school might work together toward the same ends. Accordingly, a faculty School Life Committee was set up in 1945–46 to plan the school's social activities and provide for both individual and group participation.

In 1947, the School Life Committee—composed of four parents, four teachers, and four students—set itself two tasks: to prepare and publish a school calendar and to define, interpret, and recommend school policy with regard to social activities. After four years of hard work, the committee issued an extensive report on the goals of a school-wide social program. Scarcely less important than this significant achievement was the involvement of parents and students, as well as teachers, in determining the kind of educative social life which the school could and did support.

SOCIAL SENSITIVITY

During Planning Week in 1945, an all-school study of the development of students' social sensitivity was launched. A socially sensitive person, as defined in the *Parents' Association Newsletter* for December 1946–January 1947, is one who "participates voluntarily in group activities, considers the effect of his action on others, presents his own views tactfully, listens to others and respects their rights to opposing views, has a friendly attitude toward others, appreciating their accomplishments and making allowances for handicaps."

The faculty was divided into committees, each of which attacked the problem from a different vantage point. For example, the Committee on the Role of Literature examined and annotated literary works of specific value in developing social sensitivity, and the Committee on Extra-curricular Activities studied the behavior of students outside the classroom—during lunch hour, in after-school play, in dramatics, and so on. Since the study was never completed, the extent to which it resulted in greater social sensitivity among the students could not be measured. Nevertheless, it probably had considerable impact, and it certainly led to an increased awareness of related problems.

OTHER COMMITTEE CONCERNS

The study of social sensitivity had to be shelved because of other pressing problems that faced the school staff. Once again the marking system needed revision, as did methods of reporting to parents. Curriculum-study groups needed additional time. Inter-group activities demanded consideration. The faculty found themselves constantly torn between their teaching and their committee obligations. From time to time, the pressure was lessened by curtailing the number of committee meetings, but somehow "something had to give."

The Committee on All-School Objectives took on the monumental job of determining and stating precisely the school's aims and directions and defining the basic competencies expected of its students. Using these statements as a foundation, the Committee on Reporting worked on report forms over a long period. Forms were devised, tried out, and scrutinized for weaknesses, only to be revised and improved again. When one committee grew weary from repeated attempts, a new committee took up the task and carried on. At length one outstanding fact was revealed: there simply was no easy or fast way of preparing reports for parents. More and

A fourth-grade class displays the results of its research activities. For many years training in reference work has been a part of the elementary school social studies program. A centrally located elementary library has trained librarians on hand to help the children.

more teachers began to hold conferences with pupils or with parents and pupils to discuss the contents of the report folders. This two-way communication was time consuming but highly beneficial to the pupils' progress.

FOREIGN LANGUAGES—OUT AND IN

Between 1943 and 1957 foreign languages appeared, disappeared, and reappeared in the Laboratory Schools. In 1943, Spanish was added to the high school curriculum, which had previously offered French and Latin. German had been discontinued in both schools after World War I. In 1945, French was dropped in the elementary school because, according to the *Parents' Association Newsletter,* the pupils learned only a limited amount of French in the elementary grades and the time devoted to it was needed for other subjects. Many high school students who had had French in the elementary school contested that statement, but French went out. After forty-eight years, the elementary school had no foreign language program.

That situation did not exist for long, however. In the 1950's, a movement to begin the teaching of foreign languages in the early grades arose throughout the nation. At the University Elementary School, parents of third-grade pupils were polled to find out how they felt about introducing a foreign language in the fourth grade. The poll showed a definite interest in the plan, and in June, 1954, a committee composed of language teachers from the Laboratory School and University faculties, linguistic experts, and social scientists began working on a foreign language program. Their reasons for doing so, as stated in *PN,* the Parents' Association publication, were these:

Achieving Unity

The speech organs and speech habits of the younger child are more flexible than those of adolescents or adults; the child is less self-conscious in the practice of a foreign language; and an early start and long exposure is vital to the mastery of a foreign language.

In the autumn of 1955, the experimental program of foreign language instruction was begun with the teaching of French in grade four. An entirely oral approach was used during the first year, and the emphasis was on basic patterns of language rather than on individual words. According to the new plan, the children would continue their study of French for five years, with frequent evaluations of the effectiveness of the aural-oral approach and of their progress generally.

Later, in 1959, the proposal was made to extend foreign language study throughout the four years of high school, thus offering students no less than nine years of continuous contact with one language. Meanwhile German had been reinstated in the high school in 1955, and added to the elementary school program in 1958. Two high school courses in Russian were offered in the 1961–62 school year, one for members of the freshman class and the other for interested students in the three upper classes. Four years of Russian are given at the present time.

The foreign language program in the high school now includes French, German, Russian, and Latin. An extensive library of foreign language books has been established, and a variety of audio-visual materials has been collected.

The History of the Laboratory Schools

THE SIXTH GRADE GOES TO THE COUNTRY

A highly successful enrichment program for sixth-graders, known as "school in the country," began in 1951 and has continued ever since. Each spring the entire class and its teachers spend a week at a camp. There out-of-door experiences serve to enrich a host of school subjects—art, mathematics, science, social studies, language arts, foreign languages, and music. There are nature hikes and bird walks to take, historical sites to explore, and farms to visit. Pupils observe how land is used and natural resources conserved and learn many things, including how to live comfortably and equably with classmates and teachers twenty-four hours a day.

THE READING CLINIC

In spite of the outstanding reading program in the elementary grades, there were always pupils who needed additional reading instruction. Tests showed that the average Laboratory Schools pupil was at least a year ahead of the average pupil in the United States as a whole. But in many cases a child who would have had an average score on a reading test in a public school was at a disadvantage in the University Elementary School because so many of his classmates were better readers than he. Hence he needed extra help to keep up with the assigned work. For many years, a remedial teacher had given this help. Then, in 1944, the University of Chicago Reading Clinic was established, one of its functions being to take over the Laboratory Schools remedial reading program. The next year two Reading Clinic specialists were assigned to the school, and the director of the clinic, a member of the University faculty, supervised their services. The clinic itself was supported jointly by the Department of Education and the Laboratory Schools. It has been of inestimable value not only to pupils in need of help but also to the teachers.

REORGANIZATION IN THE PRIMARY GRADES

A so-called "new" organization of the first two grades in the elementary school, which took place in 1946, was not really new, after all. Mr. Dewey had had a similar plan, Mr. Jackman had experimented with the same idea, and succeeding administrators and teachers had tried it out at various times. The scheme, evolved to give "late-blooming" children time to grow into primary-grade work and also to give more able learners an opportunity to advance at their own pace, eliminated the division between first and second grades. Six- and seven-year-old children who ordinarily would be classified as first- and second-graders made up a single primary group, which was divided into four more or less equal-sized subgroups, each in its own classroom with a teacher and an assistant teacher in charge. The children stayed with the same teacher for two years, but each year half of the class was made up of new entering pupils. The system lasted ten years. At the end of that time, the teachers requested an evaluation, with a view to restoring the previous organization. Theoretically, the idea of combining the first two grades seemed advantageous; in practice, however, there were many drawbacks. The problem of making it possible for the more able and the less able pupils to progress at their own rate had not been solved, and will probably plague teachers and administrators for a long time to come.

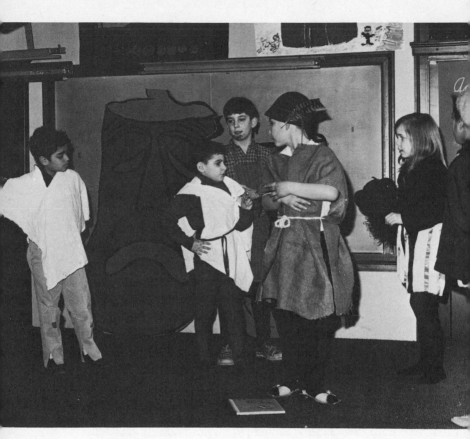

Creative dramatics at the Laboratory Schools are used in the foreign language programs and are related to social studies and to the study of literature. Here nine-year-old children play As You Like It.

Achieving Unity

Before 1944, new applicants for admission to the Laboratory Schools had been interviewed by the principals and assistant principals except in the case of kindergarten applicants, whose parents were interviewed by the teachers concerned. Mr. Gillet himself had interviewed all elementary school candidates and their parents. But Mr. Seyfert had too many demands on his time to make room for interviews with increasing numbers of new applicants. Hence the teachers were asked to assume this responsibility. Aided by two staff psychologists, they were given preparatory instructions, and in the spring of 1944 schedules were set up for interviewing applicants for the coming school year. The system proved effective and has been followed to the present day.

PARENTS' ASSOCIATION ACTIVITIES

Parents continued to play an important role in the life of the school, enthusiastically contributing to many of its projects. They, in turn, were welcome to visit classes, either informally or on special visiting days. In addition, there was the annual Open House each fall—an evening on which parents followed their children's class schedules, with abbreviated periods of ten to fifteen minutes. During this brief session the teacher would outline the purpose, content, and structure of the current classwork. Thus the parents became acquainted not only with the teacher, but with their children's academic programs.

Members of the Parents' Association had always

worked with teachers wherever and whenever requested. The Laboratory School Council was for some time composed of parents and teachers, and parents always served on the School Life Committee.

The *Parents' Association Newsletter* was replaced in March, 1947, by *PN*, an informative, well-written, high-standard publication whose purpose has been—and still is—to keep parents informed about studies going on in the Schools, the results of completed research, and proposed changes and innovations.

Another very successful and worthwhile parent activity has been the Scholarship Fund Clothing Sale, initiated in 1947 and held each spring and fall for three days. This amazingly well-organized project has been a lucrative one as well. For example, in 1956, approximately 300 women contributed time and effort to the processing of about 12,000 items. The first sale in 1947 netted $365 for the fund. In 1960, the gross intake was $5,630.86. Part of the money is allotted to the nursery school, but most of it goes for elementary and high school scholarships. The project has had a further important outcome: It has given parents an opportunity to become acquainted and to work together in a common cause.

Still another activity in which parents cooperated eagerly and effectively with the school staff was undertaken in 1948. This was a plan whereby parents reported to teachers on their children's interests outside of school, special abilities and qualifications, reactions to the school, special likes and dislikes, and so on. The information was presented early in the school year so that stumbling blocks to learning could be removed wherever possible and more effective teaching take place without losing valuable time. These parent reports became an integral part of the school reporting program, which—as mentioned earlier—involved scheduled conferences between parents and teachers.

Considering the obligations of teachers for both classwork and committee work, the curriculum committees produced truly surprising results. Some worked for several years, with changes in personnel as time went on. Sometimes, almost the whole committee membership was new, but the groups labored on.

An extensive report on students' handwriting was made in 1945. Six years later, a committee began devising an experimental scale for evaluating handwriting. This was published in 1954–55.

Also in 1945, a committee was appointed to investigate the status of spelling in the elementary school and to make recommendations. The committee not only gave tests, checked the pupils' written work, and evaluated all these, but went on to establish criteria for good spelling books. Eighteen years later, another committee on spelling made a report. Following the recommendations of the earlier committee, it surveyed the effectiveness of books and workbooks, analyzed the methods found most helpful by various teachers, and then made further recommendations based on its findings.

In 1955, the Committee on Developmental Reading, after years of study, brought out a mimeographed reading course for the entire elementary school. In the next year, the Committee on Mathematics Curriculum brought out a similar course of study for the kindergarten and all the elementary grades. The winds of change were so impelling that no course of study remained untouched for very long.

FOUR "LITTLE FACULTIES"

By 1948, there were almost eighty teachers in both schools, and all-school faculty meetings became unwieldy and time consuming. Primary teachers had to sit through discussions of high school problems, and vice versa. To facilitate matters, a new plan for faculty meetings was put into operation, designed to enable groups of teachers to deal with problems common to certain clusters of grades. Four "little faculties" were formed: Little Faculty I was made up of teachers of kindergarten through third grade; Little Faculty II, of teachers of fourth, fifth, and sixth grades; Little Faculty III, of teachers of seventh and eighth grades; and Little Faculty IV of teachers of ninth and tenth grades. Special teachers joined whichever faculty represented the major part of their assignment. Of course, all-school faculty meetings were still held from time to time—to hear a special speaker or discuss some problem which concerned the whole school—but day-by-day problems which belonged to grade clusters were taken up in little-faculty meetings.

AN OLD ORDER RESTORED

Ever since 1938, when the last two years of the University High School had become a part of the four-year University College, the high school had consisted of the seventh and eighth grades and the freshman and sophomore years. But this organization was not entirely satisfactory, and from 1949 on the possibility of restoring the junior and senior years was discussed frequently by parents as well as the school staff. Not until early in 1954, however, were definite steps taken to reinstate the two upper classes. Laboratory Schools students were once more offered an eleven-year program—six years of elementary school and five of high school, plus kindergarten. The junior year was added in 1954, the senior year in the autumn of 1955, and the seventh and eighth grades were again combined to form the pre-freshman class. Naturally this major reorganization demanded many curriculum changes and much hard work on the part of the staff, since the old 1938 curriculum was out of date by now. Extra-curricular changes were hardly less extensive. High school publications were again assumed by upperclassmen, sport competitions took on a different look with the addition of junior and senior athletes, and awards to upperclassmen were transferred from the College back to the high school.

FACULTY PUBLICATIONS AND SERVICES

The Laboratory School teachers, despite the demands of schoolwork and committee work, continued to find time to write for publication, especially the elementary school faculty. Interestingly enough, the majority of the books published in this period had to do with science in the grades. As always, many articles about the school appeared in educational journals, as did book reviews and annotated bibliographies.

Teachers also continued to give generously of their professional services. They spoke at conferences. They served as consultants on curriculum problems and on the use of such audio-visual materials as films and film

The Queen Mary—*an ambitious building program and learning experience for a third-grade class. Transportation and its influence on society were a part of the social studies curriculum.*

Swimming is a major activity of the physical education program. It is introduced at the fourth-grade level, and for the next three years almost half of all physical education time is spent in swimming.

strips. They assisted in school surveys and demonstrated teaching methods. Last, but by no means least, they were always ready to receive visitors and observers at any time on any schoolday.

THE ELEMENTARY SCHOOL LIBRARY

In 1949, a new elementary school librarian, Sara Innis Fenwick, broadened the library's services to include all grade levels from kindergarten through the sixth grade. While the earlier reading-study type of library had been effective for the intermediate-grade reading program, the teachers felt that the use of the library should no longer be restricted to this particular group of pupils. Primary-grade teachers, especially, wanted to use the library facilities to enrich and expand their teaching. They felt that children who had learned to read "on their own" should have a chance to select and read books suited to their abilities. If these children were free to go to the library for independent reading, their teachers would also be free to work with those who were not yet able to read by themselves.

To provide appropriate reading material, the librarian added a large number of books for primary-graders —easy-reading story books, picture books, and books of information about things children are interested in. She put them on conveniently low shelves and put child-sized tables and chairs in one corner of the library. Children from first and second grades came to browse, to choose books as they wished, and to read them, always under supervision, with the librarian and her assistants on hand to help.

The teachers felt, however, that all the children should have some library experience, not just those who were able to read independently. To meet this need, a story-telling program was held once a week. The entire primary group, teachers and children, came to the library, sat together on a rug, and listened. These weekly programs had many virtues. They improved the children's listening skills, extended their vocabularies, exposed them to the beauty of language, and introduced them to folklore and the best of modern imaginative and realistic stories.

In the intermediate grades, the teaching of reading was now the responsibility of the homeroom teacher, and the library became a resource center. The pupils spent less scheduled time in the library, but they were free to go there to read, to seek information, or to do research—which, incidentally, required the addition of a considerable collection of reference works.

A program for the kindergarteners was planned by the librarian and individual teachers. As a rule, the children came first to listen to the stories. Then a few who were ready to read came with their mothers, and later with their teachers, to take out their own books—mostly picture books. The kindergarten classrooms had their own libraries, augmented by books borrowed from the main library.

More recently, an interchange between teachers and librarians has been arranged for the intermediate grades. Not only have pupils gone to the library but the librarian has gone to the classroom to explain and demonstrate the use of reference materials, such as the *Reader's Guide* and various yearbooks and almanacs. Pupils studying foreign languages have had their own shelves of foreign language books, and from time to time there have been story hours in French and German.

The elementary school library is fast becoming a resource and instructional center. Besides thousands of books and periodicals, there are filmstrips on different school subjects, as well as slides and eight-millimeter films, together with four viewers. Two record-players with dual listening phones and recordings of classical music, folk songs and ballads, folk tales, and spoken poetry complete the library's audio-visual materials. In addition, a large art collection is available for circulation.

The elementary school library has had countless visitors over the years and has served as a pattern and model for other school libraries not only because of its materials of instruction but also because of the services it offers.

ANOTHER ERA ENDS

Just before the Christmas holidays in 1953, Mr. Seyfert announced his resignation, effective at the end of the school year. During his ten years as director of the school he had combined the two schools into one, created faculty solidarity, organized committees which cut across grade lines, and developed an organization of "little faculties" and standing committees that had aided greatly in the effective functioning of the school.

Harold B. Dunkel, who had been director of pre-collegiate education, assumed the directorship of the school after Mr. Seyfert left, serving one year. He was succeeded by Herbert W. Schooling.

At that time, in the fall of 1955, the school had 950 students, from nursery through high school, and a long waiting list. During Mr. Schooling's two years as director, the junior kindergarten for four-year-olds—which had been a part of the school since 1930—was replaced by a second senior kindergarten for five-year-olds. The four-year-old children went to nursery school.

In 1956, Lillie House, on the corner of Fifty-eighth Street and Kenwood Avenue, was made available to the Laboratory Schools. Dr. Frank Lillie, from whom the house got its name, was a professor at the University. His wife had been one of the early supporters of the Schools and a founder and benefactor of the nursery school. Lillie House was first used as an activity center for the high school, providing a meeting place for the Student Council, the Intramural Board, and the Boys' Club and Girls' Club. Two years later, it served as a canteen for the high school students as well as a meeting place for their organizations.

During Mr. Schooling's second and last year, plans were under way for refurbishing Blaine and Belfield halls, and there were many conferences and discussions about a proposed new University High School building

Ten

Programs and Projects, Recent and Current

Roy A. Larmee, who followed Mr. Schooling as director, had worked with the University's Department of Education for two years as staff associate at the Midwest Administration Center. Before coming to the University, he had been principal of primary and secondary schools in Michigan. Having had previous experience in school construction, he was well qualified to undertake the expansion of the Laboratory Schools.

One of Mr. Larmee's first responsibilities was the renovating of Blaine and Belfield halls. Over the fifty-four years since they were built, the two buildings had served thousands of students and served them well, but they had gradually become shabby, soot encrusted, dark, and dingy.

The University trustees had approved a $240,000 budget for the initial phase of the renovation, and an extensive list of proposed changes had been drawn up. In Blaine Hall, fluorescent lighting was to be installed, the rest rooms completely refurbished, the entire first floor redecorated, the offices relocated, the floors covered with rubber tile, and the corridors, the kindergarten-primary rooms, and the Little Gymnasium all soundproofed. In Belfield, the corridors and the art room were soundproofed, and the Girls' Club was partitioned for additional space. When Mr. Larmee made his first appearance before the Parents' Association, in the autumn of 1957, he reported that the remodeling had progressed so well that part of the Blaine-Belfield face-lifting had been completed.

At that time the enrollment was 1,092, an increase of 156 over the previous year, and plans for a new high school building were being drafted. To make room for the new building, beloved old Gym Temp, the gymnasium which had been temporary for almost sixty years, had to be razed. In June, 1959, an alumni-parent picnic marked the beginning of its demolition, and excavation for the new high school building began soon afterward.

Those who planned the building—and they included teachers and administrators—decided first on what purposes the school should serve. These, they agreed, were (1) to provide the best possible educational experiences for the students, (2) to provide a laboratory for developing and testing new teaching methods and procedures, and (3) to provide a resource center for teachers in training. Then they went ahead to design a building in which each of these purposes could be effectively and efficiently fulfilled.

Many of the suggested innovations were experimental —as, for example, carpeted classrooms. Carpets, the planners asserted, were as easy to maintain as the usual bare floors; they improved the acoustical properties of a room and certainly made it quieter. Another experiment, aimed at flexibility of space, was a group of rooms, the size of six traditional classrooms, with movable walls and sliding doors. Rooms for small groups and large could be created simply by changing the partitions. The cafeteria, too, had folding, portable walls. Planned for multiple use, it could serve as an auditorium, and on special occasions—such as Parents' Association gatherings—it could seat a large number of people.

All the classrooms were equipped for modern audio-visual facilities, with darkening blinds, a projection screen, and storage space for a projector, and for closed-circuit television. A central projection room in an adjacent building made it possible for teachers to show motion pictures over classroom television sets.

The new high school had its own theater, to be used for instructional purposes, seating 148 persons (the maximum size of a single high school class, such as the freshman or sophomore class). An outdoor amphitheater, created by the extension of the cafeteria floor, provided a place for summer dramatics and summer assemblies.

Today there is also a sound laboratory, with a private glass-partitioned area where the teacher prepares tape-recordings; a turntable phonograph, a movie projector, and a pickup for radio and television; and thirty student booths, acoustically treated and provided with earphones for listening to recordings and radio broadcasts from eight transmission frequencies.

Of the twenty-some classrooms, three are especially equipped for language teaching and research. The seven science laboratories are used for elementary as well as high school classes. A small-animal room and a greenhouse area are part of the biology laboratory, and a weather station is located on the roof of the building.

The library was designed for study, research, and independent, self-directed learning, its program correlated and integrated with the curriculum. A boy or girl can work in the main reading room, which accommo-

Fourth-grade students experiment and record data in one of the elementary school science rooms. Special science teachers at all levels work with the children in well-equipped laboratories. The emphasis is on experimentation and observation.

The History of the Laboratory Schools

dates a hundred and fifty students; or confer with half a dozen classmates in one of four soundproof conference rooms; or study alone, without distraction, in one of ten carrels. At the student's disposal are three microfilm readers in a special study area, and three typewriters.

The library now has more than twenty-one thousand books, including an extensive collection of French and German books and a growing number in Latin and Russian; pamphlets, periodicals, and the *New York Times;* reference sets, yearbooks, and catalogs—a rich variety of reading matter not only to inform but to stimulate the student in his quest for further knowledge. Also available to him are visual materials of all kinds, phonographs, and about eight hundred recordings.

The three-story building was completed and opened to students in September, 1960, and dedicated on October 27. Far advanced in school architecture and design, just as Emmons Blaine Hall was in 1903, it has attracted hosts of visitors from all over the United States and other countries as well.

Mr. Larmee, who had seen the new high school grow from blueprint to actuality, resigned in June, 1961. The principals of the High School and Elementary School, Willard J. Congreve and Mildred Thurston, carried on until Francis V. Lloyd, Jr., former superintendent of schools in Clayton, Missouri, came as the new director in 1963.

THE AUDIO-VISUAL DEPARTMENT

When Mr. Corey became educational adviser to the Encyclopaedia Britannica Corporation and Encyclopaedia Britannica Films, he established in the School of

186

Programs and Projects

Education a center for the study of audio-visual instructional materials—films, filmstrips, lantern slides, charts, maps, and phonograph records. He then began an investigation of how these materials could be used most effectively in the classroom.

At that time the possibilities of audio-visual aids to teaching were just beginning to be sensed, let alone explored. Classroom films, for example, were commonly thought of as a diversion to entertain the pupils rather than enlighten them. Now, in 1944, Mr. Corey was asking his Laboratory Schools teachers not only to make serious use of films and filmstrips in their teaching, but to evaluate the worth and appropriateness of each film and filmstrip for each grade level. Today such information is available through extensive film guides and catalogues, but in 1944 these were non-existent.

In May, 1945, about twenty-five seventh-graders cooperated with Encyclopaedia Britannica Films, Inc., in producing a motion picture entitled *Using a Classroom Film* and designed to show how teachers may make the best possible use of classroom films.

Over the years, the materials in what is now the Audio-Visual Department have increased in amount and diversity, including motion picture projectors as well as films; filmstrips and slide projectors; opaque and overhead projectors; tapes, tape recordings, and tape-recorders; and microphones, screens, and cameras. Recently the Department has been concerned with exploring ways in which the closed-circuit television in the new high school building may help to solve instructional problems.

The History of the Laboratory Schools

In 1954, the elementary school again became part of the University's teacher training program, mainly because the Education Department felt that prospective teachers were being inadequately prepared for their all-important professional work. A certain number of methods courses, without sequence, offered students very little opportunity for creative exchanges of ideas and experiences with others in the same field. In the new program, which was experimental for the first two years, practice in the classroom was integrated with educational principles and theory. The methods courses were abandoned, the elementary school itself serving as a resource for materials as they were needed. Later, when there were too many student teachers to be absorbed by the Laboratory Schools, the public schools were also used.

The teachers in training began their classroom experience as teachers' aides and as assistants in the primary grades, spending half of each day in the classroom and the other half working under Department of Education instructors. Thus the students' awareness of actual teaching problems gave their University courses both immediacy and significance. This in turn was enhanced through workshops conducted by Laboratory Schools teachers, especially those in such special fields as physical education, art, music, science, and library. And after two years the experiment proved so successful that the old system was abandoned.

The University's College of Education, which trained undergraduate students for teaching, to which the Laboratory Schools had belonged, and for which the Schools had been a laboratory, was dissolved in 1930, and re-

188

Programs and Projects

sponsibility for the preparation of teachers was given to a University-wide committee. Nearly three decades later, in 1958, the University, desiring to take a more active part in the training and education of high-caliber teachers, created the Graduate School of Education. The Laboratory Schools were assigned to the new School—once again to serve as educational laboratories, the purpose for which they had been founded.

THE M.A.T. PROGRAM

In 1960, shortly after the Graduate School of Education was formed, the University began a new two-year program leading to the degree of master of arts in teaching (M.A.T.). Its aim, the preparation of superior high school teachers, was developed in coordination with the University High School. Students spent the first year taking graduate courses in their teaching field, then taught for a year in high school, along with a senior colleague who had demonstrated success and creativity in his own teaching. The relationship between the two colleagues—junior and senior—was more complex than that of critic and practice teacher, and demanded more flexibility. All M.A.T. students were paid for their teaching.

The graduate students, called resident teachers, were admitted only after careful screening. They had to have better-than-average ability, a strong desire to become good teachers, and the ability to develop a creative, effective, vigorous leadership in secondary education. The M.A.T. program was not initiated at the University of Chicago and therefore was not experimental. What was noteworthy about it was that the University High School was again being used as a laboratory—

The History of the Laboratory Schools

its faculty, students, and facilities providing a most necessary adjunct to the new program of teacher training.

THE INITIAL TEACHING ALPHABET

Through the efforts of Helen M. Robinson, a research professor in the Department of Education who is an authority on reading, an exploratory project using the Initial Teaching Alphabet has been undertaken in one first-grade and one kindergarten class of the Laboratory Schools. In England, where the Initial Teaching Alphabet originated, excellent results in teaching children to read by means of phonetic symbols had been reported. The purpose of the exploratory project was to see how the alphabet worked with children in the initial stages of reading in a kindergarten and first grade. Having mastered the symbols, the children learned to attack words independently. The problem of mastering the conventional alphabet, and thereafter reading written English, was solved by most of the first-grade children by the end of the year. Of the children in the kindergarten class, a few made the transfer during the first year. Most of them, however, did so during the second year, when they were in first grade.

FIELD TRIPS

Since 1959 many new off-campus trips have been added to local excursions traditionally taken by various elementary and high school groups. These ventures include some fairly long excursions—to St. Genevieve in Missouri, to Yerkes Observatory in Wisconsin, as well as to historic spots in Illinois (Springfield, New Salem,

Galena, Kaskaskia, Fort Chartres, and the Dixon Mounds) and the Lake Calumet and Harbor area in Chicago. One fifth-grade group spent a few days in a small town in Indiana, living with families there, going to school, and learning what life is like in a semi-rural area. The children whom they visited were then invited to the homes of the fifth-graders in a unique, though brief, educational exchange program.

In the summer of 1958, thirty University High School students went to Europe for ten weeks. One group, under the direction of the teacher of German, spent four weeks in a town in Germany, where each student lived in the home of a German family, took part in community affairs, and even went to school. The second group, under the direction of the teacher of Latin, traveled in France, Italy, and Greece. So successful was this first summer-in-Europe program that it has continued ever since.

THE FRESHMAN PROJECT

Another challenging current experiment is the Independent Learning Project for Gifted Children, commonly known as the Freshman Project because it is mainly concerned with ninth-graders. In the words of Willard C. Congreve, it is designed to "encourage Freshman students to take responsibility for making choices about *how, where, when,* and somewhat *what* to study" and was initiated in 1961 by two teachers. These two men, one of whom taught Earth Science and the other Social Studies, were interested in developing independence in study among University High School students and in providing opportunities for learning how to learn. They set up a pilot project, in which more and more faculty members and instructional areas have become involved.

In 1961–62, about fifty students taking Social Studies I and Science I were assigned to the project; in 1962–63, all freshmen participated. Each student could choose one of three types of program under which he wanted to study. If he chose Type I, he met daily with his teacher, who planned and directed his work—specific, short-term assignments, with frequent tests and reviews. Under Type II, the student met with the teacher three days a week, doing optional work on the other two days. Under Type III, he attended one class a week and spent the remainder of his time on long-range assignments and in independent study. He set his own goals in a planning session with the teacher, who acted as a resource person rather than a director.

Optional work in programs II and III might include audio-visual activities, study in the library, discussions in group-study rooms, teacher-led discussions, remedial work on study skills, and laboratory work. Each week during the homeroom period the students made out the next week's schedule, assigning themselves different options. The cards were sorted in the statistics laboratory, and by the following Monday a class list for each optional activity was in the hands of the teacher. Thus it was possible to plan and operate an orderly program in which the students had considerable, but circumscribed, freedom.

The students were tested extensively. There were pre-tests, post-tests, and many questionnaires, but all were concerned more with growth in the skills of learning than with factual information. Interestingly enough, the tests revealed a consistent mastery of subject matter.

Programs and Projects

By 1964, the staff of the project consisted of the two originators, three experienced teachers, three new teachers, two resident teachers from the M.A.T. program, a librarian, and a member of the counseling staff. The instructional areas included mathematics, English, science, and social studies, and the types of program offered were reduced from three to two. In the following year, languages and the arts were added, so that the entire curriculum was involved in the project.

At present three other schools in the Midwest are cooperating in the experiments. Laboratory School findings and publications are being shared with these schools, and the project personnel are always available for consultation and discussion.

The Sophomore Staff Study Group, an outgrowth of the Freshman Project, is continuing to develop a curriculum which will give older students further opportunities to develop study and learning skills and to continue their independent learning.

THE PHYSICAL EDUCATION PROGRAM

From the very beginning, daily physical activity always had an important place in the Laboratory Schools program—play for younger children, organized games and gymnastic exercises for older students. Emphasis on good posture and on corrective exercises was frequently mentioned in early reports of school activities. Each year awards have been given for athletic prowess in the high school, and at least two of its athletes have won nation-wide fame.

In 1928, the forenoon and afternoon recess periods for elementary school pupils were abolished so that every student in both schools could have an hour of physical education each day. All of them, even first-graders, are taught by trained physical educators. The present director of physical education says that a student in the Laboratory Schools spends more time in physical training than in any other area except the language arts. Thus, while the Schools are well known for the superiority of their academic training, their physical education program deserves similar recognition. Actually, its true worth was unknown until the tests for President Kennedy's Physical Fitness Program were given in schools throughout the nation. For two years Laboratory Schools pupils from grade four through high school took the tests; the results were consistently higher than the national average. Hence no changes were necessary in the Schools' physical education program.

Even in this non-academic field there has been no lack of experimentation. An interesting study in grouping for physical education in the primary grades was undertaken when the first and second grades were taught together in one classroom. A very natural question arose: Should homogeneous grouping be followed —all the very able pupils in one physical education class and all the less able in another? Or should the children be grouped heterogeneously, without regard to ability? It was found that heterogeneous grouping was most effective for all pupils.

At present another study is going on, comparing the physical fitness of children who have been in the Schools many years with that of those who entered at a later stage in their education.

The high school library includes an excellent collection of books, magazines, microfilms, and maps. Audio-visual equipment is available to individuals and small groups, as are educational films, filmstrips, and records. The library has individual study carrels and conference rooms in addition to the main study area.

FACULTY CONTRIBUTIONS

A number of teachers in the Laboratory Schools are lending their skills and abilities to programs being tried out in other institutions. One of the University High School teachers, Ernest Poll, has been connected with the Princeton Project, contributing to the development of a course in "Time, Space, and Matter" for seventh, eighth, and ninth grades—a series of investigations involving several of the physical sciences and mathematics. He is also preparing teaching materials and acting as coordinator and consultant for schools in the Chicago area which are taking part in the experiment.

In 1962, an elementary school science teacher, Illa Podendorf, became a member of the Commission on Science Education of the American Association for the Advancement of Science. She has spent her summers helping to prepare exercises for elementary school science. During the winter, she has served as coordinator for experimental classroom use of these materials. Since 1964, two more Laboratory School teachers, Barbara Wehr and Heather Carter, have been working with the same group on new science materials.

Laboratory School teachers have been active in the School Mathematics Study Group, which began its work in 1958 and has produced mathematics curriculum materials for kindergarten through grade twelve, as well as materials for teacher training. Four Laboratory School teachers (Lenore John, Margaret Matchett, Max Bell, and Paul Moulton) have served on summer writing teams from one to six summers and participated in other School Mathematics Study Group activities. Experimental editions of the texts they prepared were tried out in University High School classes and in the lower elementary grades from kindergarten through fourth grade. Pupils in these same grades will use the mathematics material prepared by the School Mathematics Study Group simultaneously with the science materials prepared by the commission of the American Association for the Advancement of Science. The relationship of the one to the other will then be studied.

In 1956, a new course in physical science, developed by the National Physical Science Study Committee, was introduced in eight pilot schools in the United States. Two years later, 250 teachers were trained in the new approach and in 1959 started using the materials in their classes—new textbooks, new laboratory guides, new simplified equipment, motion pictures, tests, and paperback science books. A continuous operation of "feed-backs" from teachers using the experimental materials was carried on, and each summer more teachers were trained. One of the University High School science teachers, Bryan Swan, acted as chairman for the program in this area. In 1964, he was invited by Columbia University to serve as consultant in a summer institute at Benares Hindu University in India, to discuss use of the Physical Science Study Group materials in high schools in that country. The following year he participated in two more institutes, one in central India and the other in southern India.

SUMMER SESSIONS—1965

Since its beginning in 1940, the elementary summer school has been open both to Laboratory School pupils and those from other schools. In two summers, 1963 and 1964, more than half have been non-Laboratory School pupils.

A unique and challenging departure from the usual summer session was developed in the high school during the summer session of 1965. Three different "schools," or programs, were operated. The first, made possible by a grant from the National Science Foundation, was open to 120 students who had shown some aptitude for mathematics and science. Drawn from ten nearby high schools, the students—all Negroes—were given intensive instruction in science and mathematics by expert teachers.

The second "school" offered an English program, financed by the National Defense Education Act. It was designed to train public high school English teachers in methods and techniques of teaching the culturally deprived in the city of Chicago. About twenty ninth-grade Negro students formed the class used for observation and experimentation. Some thirty teachers received stipends for attendance.

The third "school," financed by the Stern Foundation of New York City, involved students from Hyde Park High School who were low achievers academically —and thus would be likely to drop out—but who had the mental ability to complete four years of high school. These students, selected by their school, were offered an all-day, eight-week summer session, without credit. There were twenty-eight boys, white and Negro, and they all stayed to the end of the eight-week period. The class helped to develop their curriculum, which included science, mathematics, history, art, and physical education (swimming). There was a daily morning assembly with well known outside speakers, and a field trip one day a week. The experiment proved to be a stimulating experience for all concerned; its results may well have an effect on other big-city experimental programs.

All the experimentation which the Schools have initiated or in which they have had a developing part only serves to reveal the continuing need for more. There is no end to the problems involved in the education of the nation's children, and no end to the help the Laboratory Schools, with their rich resources—of experienced teachers and nationally known educators, interested and interesting students, and loyal, cooperative parents—can give. This is the role to which the Schools have been committed for almost seventy years and in which they have performed superbly well.

Index

Index

Index

Index

Judd, Charles Hubbard, 71-74, 76-77, 78, 86, 87, 90, 92, 93, 95, 97-98, 145-146
Judson, Harry Pratt, 77

Kennedy, John F., 194
Kilpatrick, William H., 72
Kindergarten, 139-145, 180-181; founding of, 14; integral part of elementary school, 107
Koch, Helen L., 134-135

Laboratory Schools: as laboratories, 134, 136, 145, 188-190; experimental nature of, 13, 18, 19, 36, 52, 72, 95-96, 117-118, 127-128, 138-139, 199; public interest in, 16, 24-25, 28, 34-35, 101; purpose of, 19-23, 59-60, 76, 90, 183
Larmee, Roy A., 182, 183, 186
Learning: by rote, 21, 34, 98-99; child as center in, 21, 56, 59, 104, 140; continuity in, 22, 66, 84, 106, 156, 161-162; group cooperation in, 20, 22, 60, 90, 143; home economics and manual training in, 17, 19-20, 47, 77, 95, 121, 141-142; play in, 14, 79; role of teacher in, 17, 21-22, 28, 37; rewards and punishments in, 21, 143; social sensitivity in, 20, 52, 79, 86, 143, 162, 163-164; through experience, 16, 20, 34, 57, 140
Leavitt, Frank M., 93, 94, 95
Libraries, 90-92, 96; in elementary school, 108-109, 120, 178-180; in high school, 184-186
Lillie, Mrs. Frank R., 133, 181
Lloyd, Francis V., Jr., 186
Lugasa, Hannah, 103

Mann, Horace, 15
Mason, Arthur J., 46
Matchett, Margaret, 196
Mathematics, 196-197; in elementary school, 20, 173, 174; in high school, 52, 66, 82-84; in summer school, 198
McCormick, Cyrus, 39
Miller, Elizabeth, 78
Morgan, Walter, 86
Morrison, Henry Clinton, 95, 97-105, 108-109, 116, 120, 121, 149, 152

Index

205

Index

Sargent, Walter, 73, 74, 78, 93, 95
Scammon, John Young, 44
Scholarships, 159, 172
School and Society (Dewey), 19, 20, 24, 31
School of Education, 40, 42, 43, 45, 46, 47, 59, 61, 64, 73, 78, 93, 96, 110, 133
Schooling, Herbert W., 180-181, 182
Schorling, Ralph, 83
Schurz, Mrs. Carl, 139
Science, 98-99; in elementary school, 28, 56, 73, 196; in high school, 84, 197; in summer school, 198
Seyfert, Warren Crocker, 160-161, 171, 180
Sharp, Lloyd B., 111-112
Sissoon, E. O., 50
Snyder, Morton, 95
Social life, 52, 67-68, 69, 86-87, 96, 118, 122, 162-163
Speech. *See* Dramatics and speech.
Spelling: in elementary school, 20, 173; studies in, 75-76
Spink, Josette, 78
Stilwell, Katherine, 79
Student publications, 66, 126, 156-157
Swan, Bryan, 197
Summer school, 157, 197-198
Sunny, Bernard Edward, 111

Temple, Alice, 134, 144, 145
Testing, 72, 74, 75, 76, 96, 102, 103, 107, 120
Thomas, Russell, 126
Thurston, Mildred, 186
Tuition, 119; in elementary school, 26, 122; in high school, 86
Tyler, Ralph W., 146, 160

Unit and mastery technique, 97-104, 120, 121
Unity. *See* Learning, continuity in.
University of Chicago, 13, 25, 40, 42, 97, 145, 189-190
University of Chicago Nursery School. *See* Nursery school.
University Record, 28, 31, 37, 38, 45, 46

Van de Walker, Nina, 140
Viviani, Monsieur, 89
Vocational training, 92-95. *See also* Home economics and manual training.

Index